Dear Vi

May God Bless you

MY JOURNEY WITH VADAPAV

A book by

Venkatesh Iyer

Founder & CEO, Goli Vadapav Private Limited, Mumbai

Published by **TV 18 Broadcast Ltd. 2016**

Cover Image and Book Designed by **The Big Idea Communication**

Printed and Bounded by
Print Plus Pvt. Ltd. 122, Shah & Nahar Ind. Estate (A-2), Dhanraj Mills Compound, S. J. Marg, Lower Parel (W), Mumbai - 400 013.

Editor **Sheryl Dixit**

ISBN **9789384061586**
MRP **Rs 299/-** (Incl all taxes)

Printed in India
Printed in 2018

For Corporate enquires and bulk sales email us on bestsellers@network18online.com or contact us on 91-22-40019543 (Mon to Fri 10 a.m. to 6 p.m.)

Disclaimer

Testimonials

- "Venkatesh has battled plenty of odds to create a brand and a business that many had thought to be impossible. Like a true entrepreneur, he has created something of an enduring value. 'My Journey with Vadapav' has plenty of thoughts, ideas and lessons that many others can learn and be inspired from."
  - Kishore Biyani, Founder & Group CEO, Future Group

- "The Vadapav story is an exciting example of an entrepreneur who designed the perfect alignment between his product and his operating system. Hearing directly from Venky about his vision for the business, and what it takes to make it a success was a highlight for my students at the Harvard Business School. His passion and commitment to providing not only an excellent product, but a livelihood for hundreds, if not thousands, of people, was inspiring to all lucky enough to hear him speak."
  - Anita Tucker, Associate Professor at Boston University Questrom School of Business, Formerly an Associate Professor at Harvard Business School who had Venkatesh Iyer speak about the Goli Vadapav company to her Service Operations Management class at Harvard Business School.

- "During the era, where internationally acclaimed American brands and formats made their way and became successful in India, Goli Vadapav, as a totally Indian food concept, made a good headway and has become fairly popular. I wish them and Venky all the very best."
  – Ajay Kaul, CEO at Dominos Pizza.

- "Goli Vadapav is an incredible "make-in-India" success story, and we at IMD wrote a case-study to share their story with the rest of the world. There are three messages that the international audience that Venkatesh has addressed at IMD Lausanne takes away from his story: how to anticipate customer needs, when to pivot the business and what weakness can be made into strengths through smart business partnering."
  - Prof. Anand Narsimhan, Shell Professor of Global Leadership at IMD, Switzerland.

- "Venkat and I were colleagues in an earlier avatar. I remember him as a hesitant young rookie starting his career. And he was funny. I guess that's where the name Goli Vadapav came from! He epitomises the spirit of "start-up" India. And as a breath of fresh air, this start up story is non tech - in the QSR industry. Surely worth a read. If not for Venky's quotes and the metaphoric prose, simply for the journey. And the fun that he and his team have had along the way"
  - Darshan Mehta, CEO, Reliance Brands.

- "I first came to know about Goli Vadapav (GVP) in 2009 through Prof. Sonia Mehrotra, who asked me if I was interested in developing a business school case study on the venture. What fascinated me about Goli Vadapav was that it was trying to make a business that had hitherto existed in the informal sector into a high growth venture with national presence. Venky and his partner Shivadas were obviously from very different backgrounds from the typical vadapav seller, who typically operates a single outlet (in the form of a roadside cart) for the purpose of making a subsistence wage. The GVP promoters were educated and had worked in the corporate finance sector before they drew inspiration from McDonald's to set up an Indian ethnic food brand, which would offer a tasty Mumbai street snack in a clean, hygienic and convenient location to customers. We immediately zeroed in on the key challenge that the entrepreneurs would have to overcome: formulating a business model that would help them scale the business into hundreds of outlets. Venky has come and spoken to my students, and he is one of the most humorous and engaging speakers I have come across. Our case has been taught at Harvard Business School, the Indian School of Business, and the AmrutMody School of Business. It is a hugely successful case, because people can easily relate to the product. Over the past seven years, we have followed GVP's fascinating journey, including the many trials and tribulations that came their way. It is immensely satisfying to see GVP grow to 300 plus outlets as of August 2016, and we look forward to them scaling new heights in the future."

- Dr. Rama Velamuri, Professor of Entrepreneurship - China Europe International Business School (CEIBS), Shanghai. Visiting Professor – Indian School of Business.

- Books on entrepreneurship are a dime a dozen. The ones which tell the personal story of the entrepreneur provide the best learnings. Venky's story is particularly relevant as it deals with a very Indian product but applying a very alien business model- brand, quality and scale- to change the game and do it without using money as if it was confetti. Using the ubiquitous potato Goli as the medium, Venky allows the reader to walk alongside him on his entrepreneurial journey and get a real feel for both the macro and micro issues which arise and need to be conquered to be successful. Well done.

– Sridar Iyengar, Former CEO of KPMG India, Former President TiE Global

- "This book is a fascinating story of grit, determination and innovation. The very idea of converting the process of making the 'vadapav', a street food, into an organised business, spread across the country, would have seemed outlandish. But Venky and his team have shown that it is possible to chase a dream and take it to fruition. His success is truly a game-changer for the Indian QSR business and has the potential to become the "McDonald's of Indian food". Hopefully, this book will inspire and sow the seed for many more Indian food entrepreneurs"

  – Ninad Karpe, CEO & Managing Director, Aptech

- "The world is being taken over by the middle class. Consumption is the largest factor driving growth. In this context the Goli Vadapav story is fascinating and absorbing. I remember sharing my early 80s experience with McDonald's with Venky and the team. This book captures a parallel to that story beautifully. It is authentic, home grown and natural! May the Vadapav consuming world win!"

  - Shailesh Haribhakti, Group Chairman, DH Consultants Pvt. Ltd.

- "It is commendable to see an Indian Fast Food company going places by franchising its brand equity to so many destinations in such a short period. I look forward to seeing Goli Vadapav in every corner of India and create history"

– Anjan Chatterjee, founder of Speciality Restaurants Limited - Mainland China.

- "Entrepreneurship is the fine art of story-telling and the science of realising that story! A master orator and entrepreneur par excellence Venky as always has his audience, customers and now with his Book his readers eating out of his hands. A thrilling recount of Goli's - Jugaad (Indian art of the start) - Global scale innovation - immaculate execution - Frugal Brand building - proudly India's answer to the Big M! - An inspiring must read for all enterprising minds!"

  - Manak Singh, Chief Evangelist at Ascent, Former Executive Director at Tie Mumbai.

- Goli Vadapav is an entrepreneurial venture that changed the Indian gastronomical scene way back in 2004 when they opened there first outlet in the suburbs of Mumbai. Later in 2010, Goli Vadapav became the talk of many B-school teaching sessions as a Richard Ivey-ISB management case study publication. 'My Journey with Vadapav' captures the insights from the man behind Goli Vadapav - Venky the entrepreneur who believed in his dream and passionately followed to action his dream; a dream that pushed him to put the local Indian snack on the competitive global map by his sheer ability to find opportunities amongst the myriad challenges faced in this journey; a MUST read for all ....

  -Dr. Sonia Mehrotra, Associate Professor & Head Prin. L. N. Welingkar Institute of Management Development

and Research, Author of Management Case Study 'The Goli Vadapav - Fast Food of India'.

- "My Journey with vadapav' epitomises the good and the best of entrepreneurial India, made up of middle class Indians who were driven by nothing but their passion to follow the uncharted path and try their hand at something which appeared alien. The story charts the course of Venkatesh aka Venky, belonging to a community which, typically, is not associated with risk-taking, raising the humble vadapav to an iconic status. It is a fascinating story of the strategy that needs to be pursued in a VUCA world. The book is the result of the author's lectures in various colleges and other public forum. Venky is an electrifying speaker, who leaves the audience wanting to hear more. This book will be a bible for all those 'unsure' young and old entrepreneurs who wish to enter into uncertain waters."
  - Tulsi Jayakumar, Professor-Economics & Program Head, PGP-Family Managed Business, SPJIMR, Mumbai

- "This well-articulated journey is an embodiment of courage in pursuit of entrepreneurial passion, nurtured with humility. Venky and his partners prove entrepreneurship is anything but the pursuit of money. It is rather to consistently innovate, create value and make a difference in people's lives. Money is a by-product of the efforts. Every business has a story, and this one is to inspire you..."
  - Mateen Syed, Global Business Strategist, Advisor, Speaker, Silicon Valley

- "This book "My Journey with Vadapav" is a must read for all entrepreneurs, as it can help them understand the power of passion. The book gives excellent lessons on what it takes to face, manage and learn from failures, which leads to successes. This book can be of immense value to Start-up entrepreneurs who aspire to learn concepts related to pricing, promotion, and processes. The authors says 'Entrepreneurs are explorers' and I state that this book is 'Great guide which can help entrepreneurs in their journey of exploration!' I got to know more about Venkatesh Iyer, when he delivered his inspiring talk on his journey of entrepreneurship to the MBA students of SIBM, Pune. The talk was motivating and inspiring. I am very glad that this book "My Journey with Vadapav" will now be available, which will give an opportunity to millions to learn from Mr. Venkatesh Iyer's journey of entrepreneurship."

  -Dr. Raman, PhD, Director, Symbiosis Institute of Business Management [SIBM]

To Asha, Shruti, Appa & Amma. You have all stood by me through all the ups and downs. Without you my journey with vadapav wouldn't have been possible.

Index

Acknowledgements

Every entrepreneurial journey is the work of a team; this journey was no exception. There have been co-travellers, supporters, motivators as well as helpful friends and strangers. It is their presence that makes this whole experience so beautiful and rewarding.

I have many people to thank. The first and foremost is my friend, colleague and co-founder, Shivadas Menon. He has always been there for me and perhaps that is what has made each moment of this journey so phenomenal.

Bhupinder Singh, CEO, Vista Processed Food Private Limited for his unmatched support, encouragement, guidance and motivation over the years.

Ms. Raji Menon and Ms. Asha Venkatesh for not only supporting us, but participating in our journey, matching step for step.

Dr. Ram Prakash Nair has stood by us through thick and thin over the years. Mr. Jerry Rao for being the first investor to back this idea from an early stage.
Mr. Sarath Naru of Venture East came in as an institutional investor and supported us in upscaling the business nationally.

Mr. Puneet Srivastava for hearing my story patiently and helping me articulate my thoughts in the form of a book.

Mr. Brijesh Singh for the spirited and tireless efforts in coordinating to help me complete the book.

To all those entrepreneurial franchisees who built more than 300 stores in 100 cities across 20 states in India and without whom this dream would have still been just a dream...

Finally, to each and every member of the Goli team, this is the story of our journey.

Introduction

Love!

The only emotion that defines my sentiments for vadapav.

It was the food I indulged in every evening while growing up, to the extent that it became a part of me. During my boyhood days in the suburbs of Mumbai, I would stand next to the hath-gadi-wala, a small handcart loaded with piles of pav bonded together in a single slab called 'laadi'. Next to this stood the familiar aluminium dabba with its aromatic potato-chilly-ginger-garlic masala mix.

The vadapav seller or most likely his assistant invariably named 'Chotu', casually dug his hand into the dabba, shaping the potato mix into small balls - bigger than a table tennis ball, yet much smaller than a tennis one!

On preparing twenty five or so and placing them neatly on a tray, his boss, also invariably called 'Kaka', would take over. He would pick up each ball, dip it into another patila (bowl) of the thick liquid gramflour paste to gently coat it . With an adroit shake of his fingers he would position it on the edge of the dark jet-black iron kadai (fryer) that always appeared to have been cleaned an eternity ago, and would slowly slide the vada into the sizzling hot, boiling oil.

As two dozen of those yellow balls slid into the hot pool of oil fifteen to twenty hungry pairs of eyes would watch, mesmerised. They would ogle the hopping, bobbing vadas as if they were watching mermaids dance in the middle of a restless ocean, all the while impatiently waiting for Kaka to rescue them.

Only Kaka knew that crucial moment when he would lazily dip the 'karchi' (big netted spatula) and fish out the golden yellow vadas from their simmering bed. He would carefully place them on a tray, while his free hand automatically reached for the pile of pav. Plucking a single one he would tenderly split it open with his fingers, but not tearing it fully apart.

As the pav stood open and ready, an adroit flick of the wrist would see a dab of brown tamarind chutney on the inside, followed by a smattering of the red dry garlic chutney.

His next move was much anticipated as he picked a freshly fried hot golden yellow potato vada and placed it on the bed of chutneys. A gentle squeeze while bringing the ends of pav together was the crowning moment. That's when I would extend my hand three fingers outstretched, to take it from him. I always liked to be the first one to grab my share.

Resting in my hand, I knew that it would be sizzling hot and madly spicy, yet the strange temptation from within to dig into the monster and explore is too strong. The taste sensors in my head would have gone wild with anticipation. My nostrils would be filled with a confusion of aromas rising from this edible hand-grenade nestling between the fingers.

I would wait no further and the first nibble would be the discovery of the pav – innocent, bland, soft, spongy. A deeper bite revealed the excessively spicy chilli garlic chutney. Its 'Changez Khani' chilli garlic fumes rushed through the nostrils.

Getting into my stride, I would next taste the sweet tang of tamarind chutney, offering my taste buds a little solace; but before I could caution my tongue, the hot erupting volcanic potato patty still warm from its over one hundred eighty degree centigrade level, would be in my mouth!

I would hit ground zero instantaneously!

That single mouthful would contain everything - the heat, chilly, garlic, ginger, sweet, tangy, super spicy and potato - all at one go, with no reprieve! It would feel like a missile has been fired and the blast in my mouth has driven my senses crazy!

Then to add further fuel to the fire, I would mindlessly pick a fried green chilly from a greasy plate on the handcart and take a meaty bite of it.

Whatever sanity remained would be drained with that one mouthful and I would be stuck, suspended in the moment.

This would be my moment of the evening!

As I grew up I wondered: why do I indulge in this madness every day?

What magic did the vadapav have besides the taste? The place was perfectly rotten; the handcart was parked over a dirty footpath, most likely above a gutter or near a 'nalla' (drain) with a huge garbage pile hovering around.

To consume the pav, a persistent battle had to be fought with countless flies, all vying with me for the first taste trying their hardest to settle on the pav before I could take a bite.

Kaka persistently remained in a perfectly tattered condition, mostly choosing to stay unshaven for several days; 'Chotu' went even further! a further two steps ahead. 'Unhygienic' was an integral part of the package and was glorified in every possible connotation. Yet, it was so tempting!

And God forbid if by chance, it happened to rain on that day! Oh my God! The scenario would be simply 'Living Awesomeness' – a vadapav from Kaka' and cutting chai from 'Tapri', with Kishore Kumar singing an old romantic number on radio in the background and the Rain Gods showering unapologetically....

For those who may not know: 'tapri' is the equally unhygienic street side tea stall that is positioned alongside the vadapav handcart in every corner of Mumbai, like conjoined lovers. On a rainy day, both do phenomenal business.
Years later, I wondered why I never cared about the ambiance at these places.

How I kept enjoying myself for years... My family would forbid me from this delicacy, luring me with delicacies cooked in the safety, love and care of a Tam-Brahm home, a world of idlis and dosas. And yet I would be tempted by vadapav from that most unhygienic street cart. Why?

We have all seen movie buffs getting hitched to raunchy item numbers in Bollywood masala flicks. My situation with respect to vadapav was no different. Every evening I went to these handcarts demanding my share of craziness.

Interestingly, all the vadapav sellers had a perfectly indifferent attitude and didn't give a damn if I turned up at their handcart or not. They would simply keep carrying on with their business, yet I could not resist them. Why?

I often reflected on this much later in my life.

That's when the thought was born – can vadapav be given a place among the burgers and pizzas of the world? Can we have hundreds of vadapav stores all across India – from North to South and from East to West? Can vadapav become a brand?

Over time, these thoughts would consume me. After a few years they become so powerful, I started losing sleep over them.

In the academic world, Harvard University is considered as one of the top institutions of the globe. A couple of years ago I learned that Harvard was teaching our story as a case study in its prestigious MBA program. Harvard invited me to their campus and on a brief visit there, I shared my journey with the students.

This was, somehow, very amusing for me. As a small boy I was always told that if I didn't study well, I might end up doing nothing but selling vadapav.
'Get good marks or be ready to sell vadapav all your life,' I must have been told this line an umpteen number of times.

When I grew older, the expectation was that I would be a Chartered Accountant or an MBA. Instead, I managed to pass out as a normal commerce graduate. This certainly disappointed the people around me.

At that time, I was sent to a learned person for guidance. My family and friends felt that this step would motivate me into becoming a Chartered Accountant. My mentor was a CA topper and a very spiritual person, having spent several years in spiritual pursuits.

He listened to me for some time as I spoke of my thoughts, my dreams and my ambitions - basically all my confused and jumbled views of the world. Then he said, 'You have only two options – either get a professional qualification or do something so unique that they will start teaching about your work at Universities like Harvard.

He had used the word 'Harvard' specifically, and none other! At that time I was too naive to understand the meaning of his words. I simply went on with my life, perhaps following neither of the two options he suggested. Yet now, years later, when Harvard happened to vadapav, I wondered if this was sheer luck or simple destiny.

From the streets of Mumbai to Harvard, I suddenly realised that 'vadapav' had travelled a long journey, and so had I.

I had taken Goli Vadapav talks and case studies to equally prestigious institutions like IMD Switzerland, ISB Hyderabad and over 250 B-schools, colleges, Universities and trade conferences around India and overseas over the years, but still the charm of Harvard was unique, perhaps because of that personal connect.

Despite all caution from my early childhood, I had ended up being a vadapav-wala and now my journey had reached the hallowed halls of Harvard.

It is now time for me to share my story with the world - my journey with a humble snack that became a unique experience. Because if this can happen to me, it can also happen to any of you.

My company:

I set up Goli Vadapav Private Limited in 2003, a company co-founded with my friend and colleague Shivadas Menon.

Even now in 2016, we are India's largest Ethnic Quick Service Restaurant Company. Our number count has always been dynamic as we have been adding almost a store every week since the last few years. When going to press, we stand at over 300 stores in 100 cities spread through 20 states and union territories of India.

In 2013, we were the sixth largest fast food company in India by number of stores, as was published in surveys by India's leading research agencies. Interestingly, the first five slots in our category were all occupied by multinational brands - Dominos, McDonald's, Pizza Hut, KFC and Subway.
This journey is about nimble beginnings and how a passion for vadapav became our life story.

My Objective:

Every human exploration starts with a few raw emotions and when these travel beyond us, something creative is born. Those of us who are affected positively by this spark, end up creating something.

When this happens, a new kind of energy emerges creating entrepreneurs with vision and determination, which is what I experienced.

For a long time, transforming emotions into entrepreneurship was a big challenge for me. I saw a lot of other people struggling,

and it made me realize that to an extent, a great part of the Indian middle class suffers this dilemma.
I am sharing our story through this book to encourage more people transform their emotions into entrepreneurship. To take their dreams to destiny!

This is a dreams to destiny story about an idea, design, exploration, technology, operations and evolution.

Each of the ten chapters in this book hold hidden secrets to your destiny. Go ahead and decode them.

Eventually, this story is for anyone who may have a dream, and wishes to make their dream their destiny.

INSPIRATION

CHAPTER 1

YOUNG STEPS, THE JOURNEY BEGINS

There are some dreams that don't let you sleep. This story begins from those moments.

I was born into a normal 'tam-brahm', aka Tamil-Brahmin middle-class family. My father worked in a reputed transnational company and like any other middle-class household, we had many comforts, yet no luxuries. Our goals in life were clear cut -we were to do well in our studies and through modern education, become something sensible and steady.

Like every other middle class boy I was to be an IIT-ian, IIM, IAS, doctor, chartered accountant, banker or MBA working in some big multinational company at a high post, drawing a good salary. I was to have gone to the US or somewhere similar overseas, and should have 'settled' in life. Instead, I became a vadapav-wala.

Incidentally, vadapav was never my first inspiration for a business. As a youth, two powerful thoughts stayed with me all the time.

The first was, 'Can I stand on my feet in this world without a degree?'

Somehow the idea of hiding oneself behind a piece of paper, leading my life and becoming what was decreed on that paper for the rest of my life, never attracted me. The rebel within me always insisted that I wouldn't need the security of a degree when living my life.

But around me, most people did otherwise; they took degrees for security. I wanted to hit back against this mindset.

The second thing that always troubled me from an early age was people's excessive love for money. I don't know why, but my thoughts rebelled against the ideas of needless opulence and indiscriminate showing off of wealth.

To me, money was an asset to build something more valuable. Of course, money is needed in the world and nothing can happen without it, yet blind attachment to wealth is what I never liked or accepted.

On graduating from college,my first job was in a financial services company. A few years later, I moved to another financial services company as a partner. Later in 1996, I quit that business and founded a small boutique financial services firm to help entrepreneurs reach their dreams with respect to their brand, consumer and retail space.

My work involved organizing finance for business houses from banks and other sources. I dealt with several distinguished business people, including founders and some of the biggest and most powerful names in retail, banking and other industries.

At the very start of my career, I witnessed some really big ticket investments in various types of businesses. People raised money through us for all sorts of business expansions. For organizing these deals, we received handsome fees which made our business extremely successful.

But I still felt that unless this money was put to real use, it was a waste of an asset. It made me happy when people used their money to build enterprises and brands that now are identified as leading local brands and companies in India.

I don't know why I felt like that and nevertheless, the fact remains that when I had everything going for me, I gave up everything and used my money to start a vadapav company!

I also concluded my financial services business, vacated my offices in plush South Mumbai, changed my mobile number, and came to Kalyan with my dream to build a vadapav enterprise.

People are still unhappy with me about my decision and while I understood their pain, I was helpless. I could not turn away from my calling.

Mahatma Gandhi said, **'Find the purpose and the means shall follow.'**

I have always felt that every life in this world is in search of a purpose. And when we find it, we pursue it with determination, forgetting everything else. Once it has been fulfilled, we go back to looking for our next purpose. This, I feel, has been the trend in my life....

As an investment banker, something within me still yearned to do something different. I could never associate myself with the black suits and silk ties that I wore to work. I realized that I could never completely connect to the achievements of closing deals and signing contracts. The more they began to happen, the more aloof I started to become.

Then one rainy evening in 1996, heading back to office in my chauffer-driven, luxury air-conditioned car after closing a significant deal, while passing through P D'mello Road near Wadala in Mumbai, I witnessed a strange scene.

The car slowed down in traffic and besides the road was a heap of garbage. Sitting on this pile was a bare bodied child, mucky and shabby, holding a discarded chapati in both his hands in a vice-like grip with grim determination. With its jaws clamped to a corner of the chapati was a filthy, starving mongrel dog. It was a battle for a pathetically grimy prize!

That sight froze me! For few moments, I felt no sensation in my body. It was only after a while as the car moved ahead, that I regained my thoughts.

'What was that?', I asked myself.

For the next few days, each time a meal was placed in front of me, that scene replayed itself in my mind and made me lose my appetite.

A small child, sitting on a heap of garbage, fighting with a dog for a stale chapati! And I witnessed it first-hand!

That was my moment of clarity. I realized that if I were to do something that could make India proud, it must be basic in concept and have the ability to change the lives of at least some people, specifically those who are down there at the very bottom of the pyramid.

Simultaneously, I began to wonder just who was responsible for creating jobs in the 'blue collar' category in India. There were so many youngsters in society who had not even passed their tenth grade and many had not even gone to school. Where were the basic jobs that could provide a source of stable income for the poor?

In parallel, people of my age or even younger were completing a technical degree, getting employed in the IT industry and entirely transforming their lives. I knew of over a dozen cases among personal contacts, where friends, relatives and acquaintances had experienced a complete turnaround of lifestyle and fortune because they had acquired a B.Tech degree and were now employed in the software industry.

Children whose origins were from lower middle class families were now taking their elderly parents for vacations in Europe within just few years of being in a job. This was amazing! I was delighted in this positive change but now I was faced with a compelling question – what if a person did not even have the opportunity to get an education, or even complete it?

I recalled that friends from my childhood had suffered that fate. I wondered who was creating jobs, careers and a life for them. And if that was not happening, what kind of country and society would we become?

It led me to ask myself, in what area could I contribute to bring about a change? This episode was the first of several that inspired me and firmly placed me on the path towards realizing my dream.

Though I was never a great student in the academic sense, I still always loved books. Even now, I read a lot. A long time ago I picked a book titled Jonathan Livingstone Seagull by Richard Bach.

It was a fictional narration, the story of a seagull that wanted to fly like an eagle. Seagulls are smaller birds that cannot fly to great heights unlike eagles, which are powerful creatures and can fly up to the periphery of the atmosphere.

In the book, the central protagonist of the story was a seagull named Jonathan who lived in a colony of seagulls with his family. Most of his friends would be busy doing seagull things like catching small fish or fighting with other seagulls for food. These activities never interested Jonathan.

Instead, he would watch eagles flying high in the sky. Then one day he had a thought, 'What if I could fly like an eagle?'

His friends and family warned him of the consequences of trying to be like an eagle, but he continued to aspire and dream.

Jonathan would climb on a high mountain and stand by the cliff. From there he would watch the eagles fly for the entire day. The next day, he would go back again. He continued to watch the eagles for many days. His folks started calling him mad. But he still kept going to the peak.

Then one day he gathered courage and let himself fly off the cliff.

In a moment he came crashing down, falling ten thousand feet and hitting the ocean like a brick. Battered and bruised, he immediately became unconscious and was swept to the shore by the waves.

When he regained consciousness, his father advised him to forget the flying business.

'Father, I know I can do it!' he replied, and again he started climbing the mountain.

He kept throwing himself into the winds of the ocean and kept failing. This went on for days and months and then one day, the unimagined happened... Jonathan could fly... like an eagle!

When I read this story, its message hit me right away. I could see the 'Jonathan' inside me.

I came from a world where we were conditioned to believe that we were ordinary middle class people, living for 'safety first'. We didn't have the bandwidth to have 'unnecessary' adventures. Doing business was perceived as a 'big risk' game. We were told we weren't in that league, so business should be left to the likes of the Tatas, Birlas and Ambanis.

I could never understand this reasoning.

At that time I didn't know how, yet I knew that I could do it! I felt I could be an entrepreneur. May be that's why, even after landing a job in a respected financial services company (a damn lucky thing to happen to an ordinary B.Com), I needed to fly higher and at the first opportunity, I took on a partnership in running a financial services business.

This was a very significant period in my life. I saw the rise of brands like Pantaloons and Big Bazaar. Kishoreji's success had a tremendous impact on me. It was something that I witnessed happening, first-hand.

The Infosys, Tata and Ambani stories always motivated me, as well. In them I saw people who did something for people beyond themselves, for India.

The 'India' perspective has always been very important to me. Creating an Indian brand was always my mission.

While driving, we use two mirrors. Though the rear view mirrors are useful while viewing what's behind us, yet we drive looking straight through the windshield.

For me, the decade of the nineties was like driving a car. While I kept checking the rear view mirror regularly for what may be trailing behind, I kept driving forward, keenly observing what may lie ahead.

That was an interesting period for the financial industry and India, because it was a time of change. The liberalization of the economy began. The licensing raj was abolished. A new India suddenly started coming into existence. The IT and IT-enabled services industry began changing the nomenclature of the economy. This period saw the rise of private banks, insurance companies and mutual funds in India, followed by the telecom boom. Modern retail came into existence and the Sensex went from 5000 to 15000. The GDP growth rate moved from 3% to 8%.

The result was that all of a sudden, the middle class had disposable income in their hands. People started talking about a second home, bigger cars, vacations overseas and global brands.

That's when I encountered The Alchemist by Paulo Coelho, which contained these powerful words:

'You have a dream.... The dream has come in the womb of the universe... it is the responsibility of the universe to fulfill the dream.... The universe conspires to help achieve your dreams...'

When I read those lines, I was simply dumbfounded!

I wasn't quite sure of my dream, but I had a few clear cut goals. I knew that I wanted to build something that would touch the lives of ordinary people. I knew fully that I wanted to make something that could do India proud. I knew with conviction that I wanted to create something that would last beyond my lifetime.

With these three thoughts, I continued the hunt for my dream. Whenever I seemed to lose the way during my search, I would revisit stories from the lives of successful and famous people.

But interestingly, inspiration came to me from extremely disconnected sources.

For instance, India's World Cup victory in 1983 was a great motivator. I have always respected Kapil Dev for his leadership role in that tournament. No-one ever thought we could win the World Cup, but we did! In the match against Zimbabwe when we were five wickets down, Kapil Dev led from the front and created a world record by scoring 175. We beat the mighty West Indies twice in the tournament.

Now if we compare the two bowling line-ups we would find an absolute mismatch. On the opposing side were giants of pace bowling like Michael Holding, Andy Roberts, Joel Garner, Malcolm Marshall and at our end were slow medium pacers like Roger Binny, Madan Lal, Mohinder Amarnath and Balvinder Singh Sandhu. But we beat them against all the odds. That victory is a constant reminder that 'purpose', 'determination', 'teamwork' and 'courage' are more important than 'skills' and 'competence'.

Bollywood has been a great inspiration for me, specifically a few stars. My first choice would be Raj Kapoor, for his passion. When he had the big fall-out with his lead heroine, people wrote him off. There were reports that he spent all his time drinking and people gossiped that he hadn't been able to come to terms with what had happened. For some years thereafter he stayed in oblivion and then one day, he struck back with 'Sangam'.

History repeated itself post 'Mera Naam Joker'. Stories abounded of Raj Kapoor's financial woes after his dream project flopped, and the world laughed at his antics. But he struggled through those moments and churned out 'Bobby', which became a phenomenal hit. For me, the moral was that he never stopped doing what was his passion. In the process he might have destroyed himself numerous times, but he never gave up. Perhaps that's the reason he was titled the biggest showman of the Indian film industry.

If Raj Kapoor was passion, Amitabh Bachchan was confidence. I can never forget the dialogue from the movie 'Deewar' where his character is questioned regarding his competence.When the character played by Iftekaar asks Vjiay (Amitabh):'Tum samajhte ho, tum yeh kaam kar sakte ho?' ('Do you think you can do this work?')

The character of Amitabh answers, *'Main samajhta nahin, main jaanta hoon main yeh kaam kar sakta hoon.'*('I don't think, I know I can do this work.')

This punch line is followed by another great, unforgettable

one-liner:'*Samajhne aur jaanne mein bahut antar hai.*' ('There's a big difference between understanding & knowing.')

Now if Amitabh Bachchan was confidence, Shah Rukh Khan was energy. I never liked him initially; perhaps for superficial reasons. But it took a single dialogue from the movie 'Dilwale Dulhaniya Le Jayenge', to change my mind. I witnessed the magic happen as in that one moment, I saw the three women in my life - my five year old daughter, my thirty-five year old wife and my sixty year old mother, blushing at the same time! That's when I realized that in the end, life is all about energy and enthusiasm, and SRK embodied this.

Each of these people made their dream, their life. Films and acting were the loves of their life and they lived their life doing what they loved.

I had another idol who impressed me tremendously and still does to this day - Sachin Tendulkar! His love for the game made him its superstar. And that is the case with most achievers in the world, from any field. They do what they love and it becomes the passion and success of their lives. I have always felt that this is how life should be.

'The world will only connect with love, because we are all born from love.'

It took me almost 17 years to begin what eventually became my calling – vadapav. During this time, thoughts kept circling my mind all the time. **'Inspiration ignites us for action and brings momentum to our ideas.'**

'We collect a lot of information through our education system but it's the inspiration that ignites us.'

Then in 1992 I met Apooresh Acharya and he made a fantastic statement by saying, 'You are a born winner. You were the sperm who beat ten thousand others to be you. What height did you have at that time? What muscles or brains did you have? But you won! the race of life. Thus, winning is your destiny.'

As I look back on my journey, I feel, I can endorse those views. Had it not been these inspirations, I would have been yet another person from the financial industry living in a sea-facing flat, taking vacations in exotic locations and playing golf. Somehow, that was not to be.

CHAPTER 2

IDEA

CAN'T STOP THE VADAPAV THOUGHT!

The famous author, Napoleon Hill wrote: ***'Whatever the mind can conceive and believe in; one can achieve.'***

This quote has never left my head and heart ever since I read it as a young teenager.

I belong to a generation where people had their favourites and we stuck to these for years and decades. It's a different concept from present times where favourites change quickly with fashion and trends.

I had a clear list of favourites. Vadapav for a snack, Sachin Tendulkar for cricket, Amitabh Bachchan for acting, in movie 'Deewaar' and the movie soundtrack from an old Sunil Dutt film in the '60s! For years this song was my mobile ringtone, and it went like this:

'Chodo kal kee baatein...
kal kee baat purani...
Naye daur mein likhenge...
Milkar nayi kahani...

Hum Hindustani...
Hum Hindustani...'
(Forget about the talk of yesterday; it is now old; in this new era together we shall write a new story... we are Indian.... we are Indian...)

One day I began thinking of my life in the context of this song and the things I used every day. I began seeing brands in my life and what they represented, like Gillette for razors, Colgate for toothpaste, Lux for soap, Pantene for shampoo, Levis for jeans, Rayban for sunglasses, Reebok for sports shoes, Compaq for computer, Cross for pens and Blackberry for mobiles.

This was my life. I was surrounded by brands. 'But where's the 'Hindustani' in all of these,' I asked myself. In that instant, I yearned for an Indian brand of global stature to feature among these products of daily consumption.

In those days, a friend who was a senior executive with a multinational food company once remarked, 'Kuch bhi karo yaar, Hindustani aadmi desi hi khata hai!' (No matter what you do, Indians will eat Indian [food] only!)

This single statement indicated his frustration, but an opportunity for me.

I instantly sensed the potential of this sector. The most striking thing I had observed in the food industry was hygiene, or the lack of it. I felt, and still do, that the industry and its operators have to change their perception on this particular aspect. We cannot continue to operate like we have done in the past.

The other thing I observed was the extent of entrepreneurial opportunities that existed in the food industry. I don't think any other industry has created more entrepreneurs in India than the food business. From farmers to middlemen, from wholesalers to processors, from distributors to manufacturers, from stockists to retailers, from reviewers and even consumers; at every stage people associate themselves with this industry as entrepreneurs. Most of these people would sell their produce in the market on their own. The culture of degree-backed entrepreneurship in food wasn't greatly present in those days.

I was now happy that I had reached a destination in my journey. I now knew that I wanted to create blue-collar-job opportunities in the food industry, promote food entrepreneurship and push the concept of hygiene in food enterprises. I was entirely sure of these three goals. The question was, what to choose?

Because food in India is such a vast subject with a multiplicity of options, thinking about a path confuses, more than resolves the issue. Being a Tam-Brahm, for a long time I was stuck on doing something with idli.

Ironically, between meetings I would often go to Thane, Worli, Andheri and Dadar as the case may be, pick-up a vadapav to munch while thinking – what could I do with idli or dosa, or biryani or sandwiches, or some other item of food.

When my colleagues were with me, we would have a group discussion on the subject of food. We would loosen our ties and just hang around, aimlessly discussing ideas.

Through time spent at these nondescript street side vadapav stalls, we made friends with many vendors and slowly the depth of our conversations began growing. Soon they started sharing nuances of their trade with us, their difficulties, points of pain and their challenges. By simply standing and chatting with these people I gained valuable insights into how even the simplest of all supply chains in the food business worked. How procurement was organised, what kind of people worked in their kitchens and most importantly, what made their food sell?

In a few years, (yes, this went on for a few years!), we became such experts that we could now identify ingredients of their recipes. But I was still thinking about idli, dosa, biryani and closing financial deals for our business. Entering into a vadapav venture was still nowhere on my landscape.

India was changing. People were eating out more frequently. The new generation had aspirations that were different, and surely global. In 1995-96 when McDonald's entered India, one of its first and key employees was a great friend of mine. I would often meet him at their store in Bandra, and began observing how they operated.

Much later, my wife would visit McDonald's for work as her employers had a tie-up with them. As a result I began visiting McD stores often to drop and pick her up. As time passed, I couldn't help drawing parallels between my experiences at roadside vadapav stalls and the experience offered by the world's best fast-food chain. I realised that I wanted the best of both. I went to vadapav stalls for the taste of their product and the humility and simplicity of this offering. While hygiene, standards and sheer scale of operations were the attractions of McDonald's.

But I still couldn't make up my mind on what to do, to launch myself as a food entrepreneur. I knew what components and attributes I wanted in my product, but I didn't know what product to choose.

Then one afternoon I arrived near the Chhatrapati Shivaji Terminus for a meeting. Feeling a bit hungry, I started looking for a vadapav. On the far side of the road I saw a vadapav vendor, selling his wares from the inevitable hath-gadi. He was attired in an outfit familiar to people living in Mumbai – chappan-tikli-banyaan – that is, a vest with multiple holes. His condition was as usual, untidy, yet he had a crowd of people around him. Sensing the quality of the product, I brought myself a vadapav.

Moving a few paces away to pay for my cutting chai, I noticed a 30 feet wide McDonald's banner hanging from the building opposite, announcing the opening of its new restaurant in that location. The banner had a huge picture of a burger and the smiling face of Ronald McDonald, with its characteristic 'M' logo.

I looked at the burger in the photo and then at the vadapav in my hand. I realized they were similar! The McDonald's product was anything between the buns. The vadapav was anything between the pav. One was non-spicy. The other was spicy.

That one had mayonnaise. This one had chutney. That had lettuce. This had chilli.

I looked at Ronald McDonald, and couldn't help comparing his smiling face to that of the poor vadapav vendor in his chappan-tikli-banyaan.

In that instant I was reminded of Dilip Kumar's blockbuster movie, 'Ram aur Shyam' from the 60s. It was a story of two brothers, look-alike twins who had been separated in childhood. One brother went to a big town and turned smart, while the other who stayed back in the village, remained humble.

So I thought, why not make the two brothers meet? Let's upgrade the status of vadapav and make it stand besides the burgers and pizzas of the world.

I must have eaten more than ten thousand vadapavs in my life and visited my favourite vadapav locations more than five thousand times over the years. I had never thought vapdapav could be a business. But in that illuminating moment, everything became absolutely clear!

I did the maths - one could not serve fifty masala dosas to fifty people in five minutes; one could not make fifty sandwiches in five minutes, nor fifty pani-puris in five minutes. But 50 vadas could be taken out of a kadai in five minutes, pushed into a pav and handed over to as many people.

It could be done on a small scale. It required no seating, as people could pick up their vadapav on the move and walk away while eating it. Vadapav was the perfect finger food; it needed no tables, chairs, plates or spoons.

Fast food gets cooked and served quickly, usually within five minutes. Finger food doesn't need to be served with plates and spoons. Mobile food is something that can be carried away and eaten on the move, even hanging out of a moving local train in Mumbai. Vadapav was all of them – fast food – finger food – mobile food!

Besides, the youth were attracted to non-Indian foods like burgers, pizzas and pastas, and flocked to fancy looking MNC operated outlets. I felt that our beloved vadapav would be left out of this race despite being so widely available, simply because no one had bothered to increase its status to that of a brand. It had been taken for granted and none of the vendors had the attributes that could attract the new generation to them. I felt I could be that change.

In the past I had often wondered, what made vadapav so popular besides its 'convenience' factor? My mind found the answer to this puzzle on that momentous day. The vada was made from potato, a universal food across the world. It was very rare to find someone who doesn't eat potato. So many snack foods in India contain potato and they are all popular. Samosas, masala dosa, aloo paratha, finger chips, bread pakora, aloo bonda, bread roll… the list is endless.

The potato in vadapav is mixed with spices, coated in a paste of besan (gram flour) and deep fried. In India, gram flour is a popular base for several popular snacks and is thoroughly enjoyed. North India offers delights like sonpapdi and bhujia, the West has given us dhokla, in the South, Mysore-pak is a favourite, and in the East, fish is coated in gram flour paste and fried.

Bhajiya, bhajji, pakora, pakori, bonda – all these gram flour coated tea time snacks are found all over the country. Food manufacturer Haldirams runs a multi-crore enterprise using gram flour as the base of many of their products. Gram flour has strong national appeal and familiarity.

Now, vadapav is spicy, and India loves spice. Whether its Andhra Pradesh or Bihar, Maharashtra or Punjab – we are known as the land of spices for good reason!

The 'pav' is bread made from wheat flour, which is well know and acceptable across the country. And when each of these independent components come together in Mumbai, India's megapolis, the humble vadapav emerges a superstar, like Amitabh Bachchan.

But instead of the form, I visualized the content of the product. So when I was questioned on my decision to create an all-India brand, if vadapav would work outside Mumbai, I heard it as: would a combination of potato-gram flour-spice work

outside Mumbai?

This thinking brought me amazing clarity, and that became the foundation of my vision for Goli Vadapav. I feel that this was the key differentiator in my journey.

Interestingly, when I shared my idea of starting a vadapav business, the common first reaction was, 'Kya goli de raha hai!?!' (You must be bluffing!)

Others said, 'Are you dreaming?'

No one believed that I had decided to start a vadapav company, neither my colleagues nor my family. There was just one, single exception, my colleague and partner, Shivadas Menon. He heard my story and simply said, 'Let's do it!' And with those three words, Shiva bought into the idea.

Shiva and I go back a long way to the early 90s when he joined us as our first team member in the financial services business. A few years later, he became a partner. In 1996, Shiva and I branched out to form our own financial services company.

The best thing I like about Shiva is that he doesn't think like me at all. He is completely different! Over the years, I have grown extremely passionate about vadapav; in contrast, Shiva has always been equally dispassionate. I think in terms of dreams and vision, but Shiva stays grounded and talks cash flow!

I can deliver 200 ideas around vadapav in a day, and he can talk to 200 people in the same day. Perhaps it is this combination which has worked well for us. Had it not been the blatant courage displayed by my co-founder and friend during the most crucial crisis hours of Goli Vadapav, we would have been extinct long since.

If there is one person responsible for Goli's survival and success, it is undoubtedly Shiva.

Yes, we have disagreements, in fact we have plenty, we even fight; but the next morning we are back to building what we have created – Goli Vadapav.

It is our shared belief that has shaped this company.

So when Shiva confirmed he was in with the idea, there was no looking back. Our sessions at vadapav stores automatically increased in terms of time and intensity. As we now had a clear purpose, we wanted to know everything about the business.

As our thumb rule, we had a simple calculation. We knew that India's population was around 100 crore at that time. So if we could access 50% of the population, i.e. 50 crore people and make them eat a Rs. 10 vadapav once in a year, our business would be worth Rs. 500 crore. And if we made people eat the product 10 times in a year, we would automatically become a Rs. 5000 crore business.

This reasoning may seem ridiculous now, but when the world was working on excel sheets and ERP generated analytics reports, we opted to work from our gut-feel.

Standing beside the vadapav stalls we had understood that

vadapav was like Amitabh Bachchan - it would walk on its own! It had a natural pull and unmatched potential, and there was no reason why it wouldn't be liked across India. All we had to do was to first invade Mumbai, and the rest would go with the flow.

ACTION

CHAPTER 3

FIRM STRIDES ON THE PATH

What were we going to call our vadapav business? This was the first question that confronted me at the start of our planning process.

I had many friends in the advertising industry and reached out to them for guidance and help. To begin with, no one believed me when I explained our business idea. The most frequent reaction was, 'Goli mat de, yaar!' (Stop bluffing!)

I found that it was still unimaginable to anyone that we were quitting investment banking to start a vadapav business.

Nevertheless because they were friends, they would share their insights on branding and brand management in an informal way. Almost all of them said that if we were looking to build a brand, the name must be in English, which was presumed to be aspirational.

I contacted several people to help in choosing a name for our venture, but succeeded with none. Finally I got hold of my friend Bernard who ran an advertising agency, and almost threatened him that he was going nowhere until he gave me a name. When I started calling him every day, he began making up excuses and stories; so now it was my turn to say, 'Hey Bernard! goli mat de, please do my work.'

We had been looking through several English names one day, when inspiration struck me. I asked my companions, 'What would have happened if 'Nalli's sarees had been called 'Julie' sarees? Would they still have been as powerful a brand?'

'Nalli' is an indigenous name and is one of the most powerful brands of sarees in India for decades. Similarly I asked, what if the name of Chennai's super-famous 'Murugan's Idli' was 'Peter's idli'?

Everyone smiled.

I continued, 'What if Haldiram had called his bhujia 'Sam's bhujia'?'

Shiva started laughing, and Bernard's grin widened.

Vadapav was born on the footpaths of Mumbai, and the name chosen should resonate with the spirit, ethos and contours of the city. But the problem was that Mumbai's lingo was 'item, pudi, goli, pakya, rapchik' How could we discover a brand name out of that jumble?

At that point Shiva and I started having a parallel discussion on the number of 'golis' a few leading vadapav vendors of those times prepared daily, and the associated supply chain issues. Bernard listened quietly, saying nothing.

When we were nearly finished, Bernard spoke for the first time. "What was the 'goli' you people were talking about a moment ago?" he asked.

"Actually, the round raw potato patty before being dipped into the gram flour mix is called 'goli' in Mumbai's vadapav vernacular," explained Shiva. Bernard thought for a while in silence.

"Why don't you call your brand Goli Vadapav!" he said. "You can't have a better name than that," he added quickly.

The suggestion struck the right note with us almost immediately. We found the name was perfect in every way. It not only matched our circumstances, it was also directly linked with the product. And this was how our business got its name.

The best part about entrepreneurship is that as soon as one problem is resolved, another comes alive. Since we now had this wonderful name, we needed an attractive logo as well. After all, we were entering the retail business and the right logo was of immense importance.

> *'Businesses are built on a mix of analysis and imagination. But for a start-up, imagination is more important than analysis. While driving a car we mostly look through the windshield ahead, and occasionally check the rear-view mirror.'*

We needed a very strong logo that would stand out and remain distinct from others.

But instead of choosing just any attractive design, our logo must signify something very critical about our business and communicate our values.

So what would be our values? What would 'Goli Vadapav' stand for? After a great deal of debate and deliberation, we choose three aspects:

- Hot
- Spicy
- Hygienic

This, we agreed, is what 'Goli Vadapav' would stand for. We took this decision at a time when we had little clue of how this would actually happen.

But we knew that these were the features that could help us achieve what we wanted to achieve, through Goli Vadapav.

We had three powerful objectives in our mind - we were looking to create an Indian brand for mass consumption; to promote entrepreneurship and we were aiming to generate blue-collar jobs.

We felt sure that if we could attain consistency on these parameters, namely – hot, spicy & hygienic, we would be able to fulfil our three major objectives.

Those were our instructions to Bernard. Now he had to express these sentiments through our logo.

After briefing Bernard, he stated that he would use three colours in the logo–red for hot, green for spicy,white for hygiene!

A few weeks later, Goli Vadapav's first logo was presented.

Goli rode on a brand called 'vadapav', and this is what I thought about our first branding experience.

An interesting point in this logo was that though we chose a Mumbaiya name for the brand, our designers chose to write it in English. The moustache added to the big 'O' and the Gandhi cap, both represented our links to the roots, and represented the 'Indian-ness' of our story. Bernard also gave us a tagline that was a part of the logo namely, 'Vadapav No. 1'.

This tagline was motivated by our fascination for Bollywood. Besides, movies with similar titles – 'Coolie No. 1', 'Khiladi No. 1', 'Aunty No. 1', etc. - were all the rage at that time and Bernard felt that this would help our target audience connect with us.

We were happy with the logo, but soon the next challenge came to the front. We were grossly disappointed with the cost of real estate in Mumbai. Naturally with our financial services background, we were extremely cautious about our sales-costs-profitability from the very start.

We realized that there was no way we could run this business from the main areas of Mumbai. Initially we thought of raising the money to start up, after all we were masters of that game!

Unfortunately, whoever we approached simply laughed at us.

'Kitna goli dega!!! Abhi bahut hua... band kar. Get back to work.' (How much will you bluff, enough is enough, now stop!) This was the common sentiment we faced.

We realized that to make everyone understand our intentions, we would have to walk the talk. Our first decision was to shut down our financial services business. Our second decision was to get new numbers for our mobile phones. Our third and final decision was to quit the financial district in South Mumbai and move to Kalyan, a suburb in Mumbai.

We broke every contact with our old world and started with a brand new slate - 'Goli Vadapav' came into existence in 2003 in Kalyan.

Napoleon Hill quoted, **'Burn your bridges' and we did!** We invested our own savings of Rs. 1 crore to start the company. Shiva got four of his friends to form the core founding team of the enterprise, besides him and me.

So between the six of us, Shiva assumed responsibility for Franchisees, Mani for Accounts, Vijay Tripathi for Store Operations, Sujith was head of Kitchen, Vinod Dali handling vendors, and I took on the role of facilitator & coordinator.

We started building Goli Vadapav in 2003 with no office, no infrastructure and no inventory!

We decided to adopt a hub and spoke model. We agreed that a central kitchen would prepare raw golis and supply these to the outlets. To transport the golis, we needed a vehicle so we arranged for a second-hand Maruti van, which happened to be our first asset and also our first office.

We printed big bright posters of the Goli Vadapav logo and stuck them around the van, which became not only our logistics arm, but also our advertisement on wheels! And even when we had not a single vadapav in the market, the van created wonderful visibility wherever it travelled.

Next we needed a location for the central kitchen, and a friend referred us to a place in Dombivili.

Now, let me share some background here. Shiva lived all his life in Kalyan and still continues to live there. Most of my childhood was spent in Dombivili, where I have many family friends and have maintained social contacts till now. Both of us were extremely familiar and well networked within these areas. This made our life simpler while starting our business.

Now Kalyan and Dombivili are two suburbs of Mumbai, nearly 60kms from the main city, on the railway line that connects Mumbai to the town of Nashik.

Now when our friend mentioned the location, we travelled to Dombivili to see the site. It was a small 200 square feet open space in the middle of a mixed habitation. The landlord was a nice guy.

'How can this place become a kitchen?' I remember asking him, to which he replied, 'Give me an advance and return in four days; your kitchen will be ready!'

But our backgrounds in finance had made us extremely particular about paperwork. So what were his conditions for the lease and license contract? Surprisingly, this guy had an altogether different perspective to the situation.

In his direct way he said, 'Tu agar kagaz hi banata rahega to dhanda kab karega?!' (If you keep doing paperwork, when will you set up the business?!)

He advised us not to worry about any of that and instead focus on building our business. "We'll complete the paperwork in the due course," he said with a dismissive wave of his hand.

We were encouraged to meet such a warm person and four days later when we returned to the location, the structure of the kitchen was ready, as promised. What about electricity, we enquired. Our landlord immediately called his assistant and within thirty minutes, after drawing a few wires from a few places, our kitchen had electricity.

And what about water? Once again the boss instructed his assistant who drilled a few holes in the water pipeline and in a span of forty minutes, we had an uninterrupted supply of water!

While our kitchen was being equipped we were simply hanging around, gossiping about business prospects and sipping our cutting chai. Soon our first central kitchen was operational, courtesy of a generous benefactor.

Who says you don't find help when you need it?

Like a soul is to a body, for a food company, its life is in its kitchen. As we took control of our premises, we lit the stove and became a real food enterprise as its flame brightened the room.

The equipment we had gathered was installed. The raw material had been purchased fresh from the market and now chief chef Sujith took over. We needed about twenty people to work in the kitchen, with an additional six to eight for the retail stores that we planned to operate.

At first we tried sourcing people from local areas, but that didn't work. What we needed was people with some kitchen experience. We wondered where we could get those in bulk, and it seemed unlikely that there would be job portals or HR consultants who organized that sort of talent.

Interestingly, it was Vinod, one of the core team members who offered a solution. He was staying in Mulund, and had been spending time in the canteen of a well-known college. He knew all the boys who worked there and felt that if offered a better deal, most might be willing to work for us. Apparently the canteen was a large operation with over twenty-odd staff.

So we hired a tempo van and drove to Mulund. Our colleague went inside the college building while we parked under a nearby tree outside the campus, which became our first formal interview room.

As the men began coming out, we simply made them an offer they couldn't refuse. An hour later, we drove back to Dombivili with a tempo van full of our workforce.

Later I was informed that the college canteen had to be shut down and didn't restart until two months later. People say that competition can be cruel and this time we were the ones delivering the punishment.

Now with the men in the kitchen, we realized that we needed procedures to run the place. If not, how could we distinguish Goli Vadapav from roadside vendors?

So, even in that little space, we created sections for cleaning potatoes, blanching them, mashing potatoes, mixing them, making the masala, making the goli patties and storing these.

While doing all this, we knew one thing had to be perfect – taste!

We had to formalise our recipe.

The food business is all about taste. Nothing about food sells more than its taste; everything else is secondary. We now had to get the taste of our vadapav just right!

We had some very interesting experiences in that domain. None of us was a cook; our chief chef was a 'shippie', so he had spent a lot of time on the high seas. He had returned to India after working in the US for two decades. The first person he met here was Shiva, and the next thing he knew, he was managing a vadapav kitchen.

'A food company is all about its kitchen.'

When he cooked his first Chef's special vada, we realised that the vadapav was very bland, more continental or European in taste, and candidly shared our views with him. Perhaps this enraged him, and he challenged me to prepare a vada. Well, since I had founded this company, he felt I should know, right? I had to accept the challenge.

When I went to work in the kitchen, and it would be for the last time, everyone laughed and generously shared their views on my masterpiece! Some tried playing holi, throwing the stuff I cooked at each other. Now that was hell!

We had invested Rs. 1 crore in the business and not a single one of us knew how to make a decent vada!

In that moment we experienced first-hand, the difference between theory and practice. We had tasted over ten thousand vadapavs and could tell the ingredients of one by merely having a taste, yet we had never made a single one.

So who would make the vada for Goli Vadapav?

Looking around we realised that we had 25 boys in our team and each of them had worked in the kitchens of small canteens, hotels and street food outlets for many years. Many of them were skilled cooks in their respective capacity and the rest knew precisely what made food sell on the street. So in a way, we had a tremendous collective experience in our manpower.

We figured that if we could somehow channel their individual capabilities into a common direction, we may have exactly what we needed. In Mumbaiya language, a 'rapchick vadapav' and few smashing chutneys to go with it.

We worked on this aspect of the business relentlessly through the first few months of our existence. Taste! Taste! Taste! was our constant buzzword.

We had no sales, no operations, no distribution, no revenues; only Taste! Taste! Taste!

We tried countless variations, altering spices and mixes. With each day came a new experiment. And finally, we got it! We zeroed in on one recipe that we decided to take to the market.

In parallel, another very interesting thing happened in the kitchen. Our chief chef was extremely particular about hygiene, and we had told him that this was our core value.

Now the other big challenge was how to teach the concept of hygiene to our workforce, many of whom were barely educated. Most of them were well into their twenties and had rarely followed this concept through their life.

Were we asking for too much? The poor fellows had only wanted a job, money, a place to stay and food. Well, our chief chef didn't leave them a choice.

After inspecting the recruits, his first task was to appoint a barber on the company payroll. He made it mandatory for all the guys to have a bath and shave every day. They were to have a weekly haircut, and get their nails trimmed.

He took personal interest in ensuring that these standards were upheld at all the times, and the barber enjoyed no idle hours through the day. If there were any sneaky deviations, the culprit would be taken personally to the barber by the chef and as punishment, he was shaved bald. During the initial months, we had quite a few bald heads in the team.

We understood that if we were to talk of hygiene, the first place to begin was our own kitchen and in that sense, our chief chef was a great disciplinarian.

Interestingly, most of our team still works with us, so perhaps everyone understood the value of our efforts.

And this was how we met two of our key objectives simultaneously. We discovered the perfect taste and we inculcated the concept of hygiene in the psyche of our workforce.

But we had to do more, we had to truly be a part of the team. So we gave up our cars and for many years thereafter, we travelled with our team in buses. We never had separate office or cabins for ourselves; we worked from where they worked. We ate what they ate, and we made them a part of everything that we were doing to build Goli Vadapav.

This, I strongly feel, was one of the best things we ever did in those formative years. Our chef brought us the concepts of discipline, hygiene and cleanliness; while our kitchen boys brought us the true taste of Indian street food. These two attributes proved to be a killing combination for us, in the days that followed.

Once our kitchen got into shape, our next target was setting up the stores. The first store looked very beautiful, but in my enthusiasm I had spent more than Rs 20 lakh to set it up. Shiva was very upset because he knew that the economics won't work. He got Unithan Nair, a retired civil engineer of around 65 years of age, to work for us and it was Mr. Nair who was instrumental in reducing the cost of setting up a store to Rs 5 lakh.

We knew piloting the concept would be critical, so we decided to operate out of only three locations at first. We inaugurated our first store in February 2004 at a prominent location in the Laxmi Market area in Kalyan, on the way to the railway station. On the day of the inauguration, we received more than 300 franchisee inquiries!

Our second store opened at Murbad Road near the Income Tax office, also in Kalyan. We bought out a canteen that used to operate from the location, and inducted the owner into our core team. This was how Ganga joined us, bringing in his experience of running store operations on a day-to-day basis, covering an area in which we had little expertise.

At some point Mohan too joined us, and would go on to handle pan-India logistics for Goli Vadapav.

Our stores made an immediate and visible impact. We were different from the start and people were attracted to us. We were unlike the vadapav stalls people were accustomed to seeing.

Our third store was set up in Kalyan East around the same time. Among the three, the one in Laxmi Market gave us customers. The Murbad Road outlet brought us franchisees, and Kalyan East simply added to the numbers.

By mid 2004, we had almost ten stores in the neighbouring suburbs of Ulhasnagar, Ambarnath, Badlapur, Dombivili, Kalyan and Thane.

In fact, by the end of 2004 we found out that a duplicate Goli Vadapav store had begun operating in Ulhasnagar. When that happened, we knew we had created an impact!

It was important for us to test the format of our design, which included three critical components – Central Kitchen, Logistics and Stores. Once all three were working well in tandem, we were ready for the next stage.

CHAPTER 4

CHALLENGES

POTHOLES AND PITFALLS ARE A PART OF LIFE

By the end of 2005, we had added over twenty stores to our chain. Three of them were self-owned, and the remaining were franchisee stores.

Of course, everyone was extremely delighted. We felt elated. People now recognized us as real vadapav-walas.

We had a rule, every evening we would have a core-team huddle in the office. The kitchen guy, the vendor management guy, the accounts guy, the store operations guy, the franchisee in-charge - everyone would pool in their thoughts together during those sessions. Every day we would visit a store and see the crowd buying vadapav.

On those trips, it seemed as if everything was perfect. The sales were superb, the consumers were happy, the franchisees were making money, new franchisee inquiries were pouring in and yet, something bothered me.

It made me wonder, if growing this kind of franchisee-based business in the food industry was so simple, why hadn't big business houses ventured into this area until now.

If one could put in a central kitchen, hire a few boys, design the logistics and organise stores, anyone could have a food brand! It was all too easy. So how come the Tatas, Birlas, Ambanis, Mahindras and Godrejs had such a minimal presence in the food industry?

I had to know why? And I was forced to ask myself, was this business really as simple as it looked?

Our journey till then had been essentially smooth on both, the expansion and sales sides. But I felt very strongly that I was missing something, I wasn't seeing the whole picture.

Interestingly, while our operations were progressing, we were confronted with a unique incident.

One fine morning on arriving at work, our people discovered a paper pasted on the shutter of our central kitchen. It was a notice from the local municipal corporation seeking an explanation for operating an illegal commercial kitchen.

We took the notice to our friendly landlord saying, 'Look at what the municipality is demanding about your premises?'

He didn't even bother to look at the paper, instead he remarked, 'Who said those were my premises?' And he walked away!

We were left staring at each other in shock. At that moment we realised that for months we had been running a legal business from illegal premises using a fake electricity connection and unauthorized water supply.

We finally understood why our erstwhile landlord was such a big supporter of budding entrepreneurs.

Fortunately that space was proving too small for our growing business and we had already been making alternate arrangements. We had put up a G+1 (5000 sq. ft.) building at another location in Dombivili, at a capital investment of Rs. 50 lakhs. This was where we eventually moved our central kitchen which now houses our formula plant and central cold room. And no, we don't receive any notices for breach of any local laws! By sheer coincidence this new location was called 'Golavly' in Marathi and by default, spelled 'Golivalley' in English!

A banker who came to inspect the facility commented that like Silicon Valley revolutionized the IT world, the QSR revolution of India would happen in Golivalley!

Our central facility was now transformed into a robust infrastructure, including staff quarters, washrooms and the kitchen. It could accommodate fifty people.

Once our central kitchen was up and running, I wondered how many similar facilities we would have to create if we were to serve all of Mumbai. I had pan-India ambitions from the start and began to contemplate on the number of such kitchens that would be needed if Goli Vadapav was to be introduced in say,100 cities.

Now our original small (but illegal) facility was good for three stores; this new one was perhaps good to support forty stores; but what thereafter?

My mind began to obsess on these thoughts and I began to feel that sooner or later, we would have to pull down our own creation in the greater interest of going national and becoming a pan-India brand.

I decided not to share my thoughts with anyone at that point, to avoid confusion and uncertainty. Everyone was so happy that we had created an effective infrastructure for vadapav. But I knew intuitively that this structure was only short term.

Shortly after, my fears proved correct. The real truths of the trade began emerging. On the stores side, as we started dealing with franchisees, we began discovering new domains of relationships. For instance, we had a franchisee who was in the habit of drinking. He would start hitting the bottle at around 9:30p.m. or 10p.m. every evening! At 10:30p.m. our logistics in-charge would receive his first call in which the franchisee would be drunk and abusive. By 11:30p.m. our operations in-charge would receive his call. By 12:30a.m. Shiva's phone would ring and around 2:30a.m., he would call me! Our entire team would be targeted by a series of calls! The fellow would be completely out of his senses and totally unapologetic.

But the first thing next morning, he would be in Dombivili falling at our feet and begging for forgiveness.

We had no clue about what to do with that fellow!

The other franchisees too, would have their own complaints.

When we looked at their business from their perspective we realized that they were making money on every vadapav they were selling. We took care of all the hassles for them, but they still complained. Why was the disconnect between our teams and franchisees growing?

If the design of the business is seamless it will grow, otherwise it will struggle.

Relooking at our growing business, I realized that our design was deeply flawed and I could sense its shortcomings.

The first and the most serious worry was that our design resulted in tremendous wastage of the raw uncooked product. This was because our product had barely any shelf life. At the most, it could last 10 to 12 hours post production in the central kitchen. As a result the 'golis', once delivered in the morning by the delivery van, would start turning stale by late evening.

The initial fight between us and the franchisees was about who would take on those losses? The franchisees felt it was our fault and our people said, since it happened in their premises it was their fault; their storage facility wasn't properly organised.

The result was that we were wasting almost 3000 golis each day and no matter who owned the responsibility, the fact remained that our product had no shelf life.

> *'It is the design of the business that makes it or breaks it. Most businesses fail because the design is poor.'*

This was a huge loss.

Next, our product was easily prone to pilferage. Anyone could conveniently modify it in size and quantity. They could pull out small quantities from each 'goli' and turn it into an extra one.

The third problem was within our kitchen and we learned about this from our customers. People said our product would frequently change in taste. On investigation we discovered that whenever a member of chef's team went on leave or had a day off and a new guy replaced him in the task of making the masala mix, the taste would change.

This meant our product was person-dependent for taste and quality, and had no standardization.

This exposed us to a huge lacuna, a major shortcoming in becoming a brand. Can you imagine Coca Cola or Britannia biscuit tasting different in each bottle or pack? If we were to be a brand, we had to ensure uniformity in taste and our product had to have a consistent standard.

We felt we were doing everything correctly, in fact, perfectly. We had a well-organized central kitchen where we made patties using trained manpower enforcing SOP (Standard Operating Procedures), and using the best possible hygienic methods.

We had separate sections for every activity and though there was no automation, our facility still worked like an assembly line production. We had strict quality control procedures that were enforced religiously. Our logistics were also almost perfect.

We put our raw patties in clean trays and stacked them neatly in the delivery van. Each tray had a specific number of patties, these were never overloaded or under-filled. We ensured the trays reached the outlets in minimum possible time. We had a daily delivery schedule for every store, and took extra care to make sure we stuck to this.

Compared to some of the other operators, we realized that they weren't doing even half of what we were managing. And yet we were facing challenges which the outside world knew nothing about.

We had one more major worry, our product had an almost negligible margin. The selling price was static; in fact we had already sold our product for a rupee higher than the rest of the market, citing better hygiene, quality and brand as the key reasons.

As a result, whenever there was an escalation in the prices of raw materials like potato, gram flour, spices and oil, it would adversely hit our profitability.

Though our franchisees were making money on every vadapav they sold, in contrast we were losing money on every vadapav delivered to them, and that was killing our business.

We had already worked out a line of credit from a bank, impressing them with our fantastic run in signing twenty odd franchisees and showing superb sales in three company owned stores. Now the same bankers were after us, questioning the logic of our business.

Towards mid-2005, our bankers suggested that we didn't have a viable business. Later in early 2006 they gave us a final ultimatum and notice that we must either come out with a purposeful plan that would improve our financial health, or terminate the business within the next 10 days.

By then we had accumulated a substantial debt with the bank. Interestingly, our sales were still fantastic and in fact, growing. We had more franchisee inquiries than ever before. But our bankers saw no logic in our business model. They advised that we would continue to bleed more and more, even as we grew.

By this time, we were also left with no savings as we had put all our money into the business. And we had little idea of how these issues could be handled.

But because it had been our choice to be vadapav-walas, we were not willing to give up yet.

Learning of our financial condition, an acquaintance remarked, 'Venkat, vadapav won't become a burger, though in the process you look sure to become a beggar!'

And while most of our friends and associates were taking their families on vacation to places like Montreal, Munich and Macau, we didn't even have the money to take ours to nearby Matheran!

The strangest irony was that from the outside, everything still looked great. The stores had excellent customer traffic, franchisee inquiries continued to multiply and people liked what they were eating at Goli Vadapav. They had begun relating to the concept of 'Hot, Spicy & Hygienic', yet a different story was unfolding behind the scenes.

We kept our internal condition a strictly guarded secret, even within the team. So except for Shiva, our bankers, our auditors and myself, everyone knew only what they saw at the outlets.

Our bankers began following up with us every day but never for a moment did we think of quitting. Perhaps this was madness, but maybe madness was what we needed at that hour.

We acknowledged that we had a few problems, namely:

1. Cash;
2. Wastage;
3. Pilferage;
4. Frequent variation in taste (non-standardization in product);
5. No cushioning against frequent price fluctuation of raw materials;and
6. Partner relationships

This was how we interpreted the message from our bankers and realized that if we could fix these six things, our business could still grow and be successful.

Once we decided to take the plunge, we made a few swift decisions. Shiva took responsibility for the Cash and Partner Relationships while I took responsibility of the product related challenges. We said 'the show will go on', without even knowing how.

In the coming days, we tossed around several rounds of ideas. One line of thinking was that we should add more products to our pipeline. It was suggested that we could bring in products like biryani which offered higher margins that could possibly help improve our bottom line.

Another thought process was that we could start diversifying into the catering business, since now we had a fantastic central facility. We could take party orders and turn into full time caterers, building a roaring business.

A third line of thought was that we could begin running college and office canteens. With vadapav as a base product, this could have been an excellent option and the people we contacted for guidance even gave us leads to potential customers and a few open opportunities in this area.

So we gave the last option a try as well. We began running the works of the canteen in a large public sector entity where almost five thousand people worked. But that engagement didn't go beyond a few days, for unavoidable reasons.

We were also confronted with a few legal challenges, to add to the rest. One came from the Octroi department and the other one because of one of our van drivers. In both cases Dr. Ramprakash Nair, an eminent social worker and a law expert, helped us out.

Thankfully those issues made us understand that logistics was a specialized area and that we needed experts specific to that domain, to run that area of our business.

This made us realize that we had to make a choice between either continuing the vadapav business or being delivery people. We figured out that we couldn't be both.

When working out the cost of operations, we realized that there had been multiple cases of fuel theft, breakdowns, unnatural repairs and other issues despite constant monitoring and surveillance.

We had merely twenty stores all within twenty kilometers driving distance from the central facility yet by now, facing logistics-blackouts was not an exception. It made me wonder what would happen when we began pan-Mumbai and later pan-India operations, doing distances of maybe 2000 kilometers every day.

It's a fact that today we actually do 2000+ kilometers in 5 different directions, from Mumbai to Delhi/Punjab; Mumbai to Gorakhpur; Mumbai to Kolkata; Mumbai to Chennai; and Mumbai to Cochin.

Clearly our logistics set-up was not adequate to support long-term growth. It definitely needed changing. So here was another challenge to add to our increasing list of challenges!

We also began thinking of outsourcing specific tasks within our value chain to specialist partners.

The final piece in our jigsaw of challenges occurred when one day, a stone appeared in one of the golis. It became an enormous issue.

Instead of calling one of us at the front end of the value chain who were responsible for relationships, the franchisee directly called the kitchen.

Shiva, myself and our senior team were elsewhere on that day and found out about the incident only much later.

So when the call went to the kitchen, one of the boys faced the franchisee's ire.

Now our kitchen was like a cantonment in terms of discipline, and yet it had a very relaxed atmosphere. Our chef allowed no nonsense at work, but otherwise the boys were reasonably free to express themselves. But none of the people in the kitchen had ever interacted with the franchisees and were not trained to use the poise that is expected when communicating with business partners.

So when the franchisee called and began expressing his sentiments about the product and the brand, the boy answering the phone seemingly replied in a casual tone, 'Panch rupay ke vada mein patthar nahin to kya heera milega!' (In a vada that costs five rupees, you can expect to find a stone... did you expect a diamond?)

This statement brought the whole business to a standstill as the message spread like wildfire from one franchisee to another.

As soon as we found out what had happened, we rushed into damage control mode, cooling tempers at both ends. Finally the franchisee demanded that if the erring boy personally apologized to him, he would let go of the matter. I took our boy to the franchisee's outlet to render a formal apology and close the issue.

But when we reached the franchisee's store, he had already gathered a big crowd which included hefty-looking people with thick gold chains and large rings in their big cars who were flashing flags and stickers from varied political outfits. I was quite sure that a few were even armed! Other franchisees were also in the crowd.

In contrast, just the boy and me had gone there on a scooter, trying to keep the matter private.

I had a strong premonition that I should call the team but there was no opportunity to do so.

Well the boy apologized, touching the franchisee's feet.

> *'Micro and macro is the same; that's why the solar system looks like the replica of a tiny atom. Scale means replicating a perfect unit again and again.'*

Unfortunately instead of accepting the apology, our partner chose to use the moment to flaunt his own agenda and started berating us.

He got up from his chair and began a kind of mud slinging spree, while his guests listened. Now this guy was more than six feet tall and big-built. He carried on humiliating and insulting us for some time. I admit that I had no clue what to do. I hoped he would soon get tired of his own antics and the sound of his voice, and stop.

But he went on and on and suddenly something completely unimaginable happened.

Our boy, barely over five feet in height, lean and thin as most young workmen are, stepped up and slapped the big fellow real hard on the cheek.
Everyone was stunned!

Then turning to me he said, 'Sir, throw me out of the job, that's acceptable, but I won't listen to this nonsense anymore.'

In the meantime the franchisee recovered from the shock and started off on a bout of fresh slandering. Our boy stepped up once again and this time, slapped the other cheek even harder!

Oh my goodness!

I won't explain how we escaped from that situation that night.

But about two months later I ran into the franchisee's brother, a qualified finance professional and someone most unlike him. He told me that since the episode, his brother has been taking advanced treatment for acute depression from one of Mumbai's top physicians. I felt truly sorry on hearing that and I wished him a swift recovery. What else could I have said?

For me, irrespective of the outcome we had lost a store and

business for a week at a time when every number counted. We had lost money, when we had little to lose.

But the good news was that by now we were aware of most of the challenges of running a food-chain business in India. We had no clue as to what the solution to each of them might be, but we had made a start!

EXPLORATION

CHAPTER 5

NEW SIGNPOSTS, NEW INROADS

We have now covered the challenges faced by the Vadapav team on reaching the mark of twenty stores. Now let's explore how we overcame each of these challenges.

Among our set of six major challenges, the first that we handled and at the fastest pace, was our relationship with our franchisee partners.

I can't say why but the 'slapping' incidence created a mysterious kind of impact for both parties, resulting in uncertainty. We could sense an underlying fear on both sides.

So we used this as an opportunity to inject a wave of positivity into the system.

We reached out to all our partners on a one-to-one basis, talking to them directly. Most of our partners confessed that working with us had been a good experience for them, and that they would like to continue the relationship.

We felt great reassurance that perhaps both sides had learnt their lessons from the experience.

Now as co-founders with clearly defined roles, I set forth to solve the problems of wastage, pilferage and standardization.

I took on the role of explorer, while Shiva took charge of the operations. He would ensure the show kept running until I found the solution to our problems.

Now an explorer usually begins his quest based on a gut feeling and my situation was no different. I had no clue about how any of our problems could be managed, but I knew that somewhere in this big world was a solution for each. I simply had to find them.

That's when I recalled what my father used to often say. He worked for a transnational company that made the world's most popular toothpaste. When people quizzed him why his company rarely introduced variants to its products or why it wasn't known for other FMCG products like soaps, detergents, etc., he would invariably say that his company manufactured only one toothpaste and that was the world's best toothpaste!

This statement made me think - what would make our vadapav, the best vadapav in the world?

It was a crazy thought, yet tremendously motivating and I promised myself that I was going to create the most astonishing vadapav of the world!

Yes! Explorers are often unrealistic in their assumptions. But they have to be; or they will never be self-motivated.

I also adopted another analogy: light if focused, could cut through steel. That's when it's called laser. I quote this line because at that point, I felt we had gathered the basic material to create the energy to cut steel. All that was needed was the right piece of technology.

I truly felt that through our experiments which had brought us to the level of twenty stores, we had created an excellent chance of making a big difference to not just vadapav, but the entire ethnic food industry!.

I have no idea what brought about this confidence, but I feel that it was always there!

And that's why I constantly opposed every idea and thought of diversifying into other food operations or businesses. My vision was that we should risk being a single-product-national-chain, rather than become a 200-products-Kalyan-chain.

I firmly believed in this principle and felt amazingly confident that this is how it should be done. Because if there were six cups of tea and just one spoon of sugar, I would prefer putting it all in one cup.

So, energy, money and time are consolidated into one single idea!

That was my message to myself as well as the team. We needed to focus! focus! focus! And I kept thinking vadapav! vadapav! vadapav! How can we make the best vadapav with a definite shelf life, which cannot be pilfered and is as standardized as any other top branded product?

I had no available resources like books or research, nor the cash in hand to consult renowned food experts. The few I had spoken to had little experience in vadapav and unanimously suggested diversification. Yet I was exceptionally clear about focussing on vadapav at all times.

I felt no fear of what may happen, because I was determined to find the solution to our problems.

Meanwhile in parallel, Shiva was having his own experiences. In the operations role, his priority challenge was to find cash to run the business. Since the bank was not supporting us, my co-founder devised his own ways of raising funds for the working capital.

Incidentally, if my partner has ever claimed credit for anything in life, it has been for his impeccable record of collecting donations for the annual Ganeshotsav festival to support various Ganpati mandals all over Kalyan. He claimed that he could get money from almost anywhere! For years he had collected donations in every sort of denomination and from all kinds of people. At that point he brought that skill to Goli Vadapav.

One day I was asked to interview a person for a senior level position in the company. I felt surprised, because we already had an equally senior person holding that position, and we had not discussed creating a parallel seat for that role.

'Just interview him,' Shiva said abruptly, en route to somewhere else.

On reviewing the candidate's papers, it had a copy of his 'would-be' employment contract. As I went through it, I was surprised by the details.

He was giving us a Rs. 15 lakh deposit for being an employee of the company!

Later I questioned my co-founder, but he was absolutely cool about it. He said it was a practical arrangement. The poor guy had returned from somewhere overseas and was unable to find a proper job matching his qualification. We were willing to hire him, but needed surety from his side, since his role would allow access to most of our proprietary secrets, which resulted in the security deposit.

I was still sceptical and asked Shiva to give the decision a second thought. His response was blunt. "Money is money, whether you borrow it from a bank or a person. This money was being taken for a purpose, and there is nothing wrong in that. Besides, my solution is better than going to the money sharks in the market," he stated.

That effectively shut me up!

Shiva has an extremely pragmatic approach to many things, which I have always admired.

On my part, I continued my search for a solution to our woes of wastage, pilferage, standardization and protection from frequent price fluctuations. And I had a strong feeling that a lasting solution could be found only through technology. Now who could think of technology in relation to vadapav?

So I looked at associated industries and other food items for inspiration. My father worked in a company that made toothpaste, and I knew someone who made the machine that made toothpaste! So I reasoned, if toothpaste could be made by a machine, why not vadapav?

With this thought in mind, I began meeting several people who dealt in those kinds of machines. I started ideating with experts who made machines for potato chips, processed food items, ice creams and similar products. I would meet them after work hours and mostly on personal terms, since we had no money to engage their employer company in finding us a solution.

I picked up tips from them, and would carry out small experiments. We even went on to design and assemble a few prototypes. But when we tested them in our kitchen, most failed.

Yes, all my experiments led to just one destination – failure! I must have talked to over thirty technology experts and tried two dozen ideas, including several 'jugaads'. But they all failed, one after another.

I refused to give up and kept looking for alternatives. I immersed myself in books on instrumentation engineering, food technology and associated fields.

The task was an extremely laborious exercise, but I didn't lose faith, not for a moment.

Six months went by and my co-founder had started pawning gold. I would go through periods of sheer terror, but whenever we started running out of cash, an amount from somewhere would show up on our bank statement.

The first time I asked him where the amount came from, his answer was terse, "Wife's gold," he said. The next time it was, "Sister's gold." The time thereafter it was, "Sister's neighbour's gold!" I stared back at him grimly, so he added, "The guy is a great entrepreneurship enthusiast!"

Until then I had only heard stories of the passion that drives people which would take them to the heights of madness to reach their chosen objective. On encountering these episodes at Goli Vadapav, I discovered that we had been bitten by the same bug.

> *'Evolution always happens on the verge of extinction. Larva becomes caterpillar; caterpillar becomes butterfly.'*

Shiva continued to collect funds from almost anyone and everyone he came across, which even included an auto rickshaw driver from Kalyan whom he had known for years.

While all this unfolded in the backdrop, on the front end we didn't let our sales drop. We worked on repairing our relationships with our franchisees and improved our supervision in the stores. To protect the brand, we added wastage and price fluctuation risk to our books.

As the cash kept pouring in steadily, I kept expanding my exploration. I often quote this example: Vasco da Gama discovered a sea route to India and he was always called an explorer. But it was the British who came and set up the empire. Alexander the Great as he was called was a great conqueror, yet it was the Romans who built the empire.

It is fortunate that we understood what enterprise building was all about: building an empire, yet the route for that empire begins with exploration.

Our empire building happened between exploration and operations.

I began thinking that if other companies in the food business could find solutions to the problems of wastage, pilferage and standardization by using technology, why couldn't we?

And if technology could increase the shelf life of food items like idli, rasgulla and gulab jamun, why not for vadapav?

I kept studying alternatives and kept exploring options and we shortlisted three technologies, namely

- Nitrogen Gas Chambers
- Ultra Violet Radiations
- Blast Chill Refrigeration

This is why we had to pawn gold when our sales were improving; to meet the needs of these explorations. Nothing in this world is free. The money we borrowed was used to explore in these efforts.

Personally for me, things moved to a different level at this stage. The moment I stepped into the kitchen, the boys would start murmuring, "Scientist alla!"(the scientist has arrived.)

No one could understand why so much experimenting was needed for something as simple as a vadapav.

I had been using ad-hoc consultancy from experts in the fields mostly after their working hours and on meeting a friend at his home one day, his wife bluntly told me to not come to their place anymore.

She did not mince her words, saying that I had lost my mind trying to make a machine for vadapav and should spare her husband, lest this insanity infects him as well.

At my home, my father was surprised to see me reading books on engineering. "Had you studied as much at the appropriate time, you would have at least become an Engineer!" he said.

Despite all these setbacks, I kept making the effort and continued to seek a solution to our three core problems. But nothing seemed to work in totality. There was no comprehensive solution that would fit our requirements.

So our experiments were failing and with each failure, we were losing money. We had exposed ourselves to a double whammy!

Word started spreading on the company grapevine that we were facing a huge financial crunch. Many of our colleagues felt increasingly worried about their jobs and future.

But at this point, we hit on a partial solution to our problems; one that could be set up in our kitchen. I also realised that it would be good enough to take us to the level of forty to fifty stores.

But that was not enough for my ambitions; I realized that we needed far superior technology which might be beyond our scope.

It happened that on one afternoon in 2006, a formal letter from the bank arrived, offering us 10 days notice to close the business. The bank in turn, would have to forfeit our assets to recover its dues.

Surprisingly, neither Shiva nor I felt any fear. Yes, I felt a little lost, but I still believed that what we desired was possible. I told Shiva that I was going home early and on reaching my residence, I decided to go for a swim.

When I reached the clubhouse, I dived into the pool and did a few quick laps. My mind continued to dwell on the solution to the three problems. I mulled over how the partial solution could be turned into a comprehensive solution. I wasn't thinking about the closure of business; but instead, what would work. Perhaps people were right, I had gone completely insane!

Suddenly it began to drizzle, and on looking around I saw a canopy near a corner of the pool and rushed to shelter under it. Also sheltering from the rain was a middle-aged Sardarji. Since there was nothing else to do besides wait for the rain to stop, we exchanged friendly smiles and courteous greetings. After a moment, my companion asked, "What do you do?"

Now as if I had been waiting for that question, I began with my story. I explained how we began making vadapavs and completed my narration covering details of my experiments with technology in the quest to create a machine for vadapav. I unburdened the story of my journey without thinking. Perhaps I just wanted to talk about it. I don't know but I may have said that I was somehow missing the right technology or the right button, and needed help from someone.

Through my narration, my audience listened to me with absolute patience. By the time I was nearly finished, the rain had stopped. My listener stood up but just before leaving he gave me his mobile number and said, "Call me at ten tomorrow morning." His last words to me standing in my swimming trunks was, "Maybe I can help!"

I had no clue about who he was, and how he could help.

Well, the next day I called my new friend and met up with him. A day later, he visited our central kitchen to see our operations, followed by store visits at which he saw the huge crowd outside each of our stores.

The next day, he invited us to his office in Taloja, an industrial township on the outskirts of Mumbai. Only on reaching his office did we comprehend exactly where we were.

We were in the headquarters of Vista Processed Foods, a joint-venture between OSI Inc. USA and McDonald's Corp. USA, and the sole supplier of burger patties to McDonald's in India.

Who says miracles don't happen in life? That day I met a likeness of God in Bhupinder Singh!

I was a finance professional with a passion for food, but with no knowledge of food technology. In contrast, Bhupinder Singh knew only about food and its technology.

'Assets of true utility are mostly developed in small parts and in different places. Rubber originated from South America; major oil reserves are held in the Middle East and the combustion engine was invented in Europe. When brought together, they make a car.'

He was an engineer from Punjab University with an impressive career. He had to his credit, the bringing of instant noodles to India and making them a big success. Following that he had helped another MNC launch a leading brand of potato chips, and a famous tea-time snack. Now he was heading Vista Processed Foods that was assisting McDonald's set its footprint in India.

Bhupinder Singh was passionate about three things: food & food technology; the Indian food industry; and ethnic Indian products.

Bhupinder Singh happened to us when we were weighted down by a pile of failures and Vista Processed Foods happened to us when we had nearly reached the point of extinction.

A week later we told our bankers that we were applying to enter into a supply chain contract with the world leaders of frozen processed foods. We explained that we would now outsource all our production and logistics to this professionally competent entity, and restrict our focus to retail operations and brand building.

Up until then I had only heard of the term called 'paradigm shift'. I had seen it happening to others like the Biyanis of Future Group. But when we signed on the dotted line with Vista Processed Foods, I realized that it had happened to us.

So now the entity that was supplying raw burger patties to McDonald's in India would supply raw vadapav golis to Goli Vadapav, with everything manufactured on a completely hands-free HACCP certified plant using world-class IQF (Individual Quick Freezing) Technology, where every vada would compulsorily pass through X-ray screening and a metal detector.

I knew we had come a long way!

I have heard that when you touch your core and ask the purpose of your existence, God tells you your destiny. It was then that I revisited the journey that had gone into the making of my destiny.

Thanks to my father who worked in a transnational company, I knew what contract manufacturing was from an early age. So when the talks with Vista began, I could understand what they were proposing and could manage the conversation effectively; perhaps this is what they liked.

The only deviation in our case was that unlike larger companies with huge brands and a small contract manufacturer, our brand was the reverse – small, with a huge contract manufacturer!

The CEO from Vista resided in my neighbourhood and unknown to me; I simply continued solution seeking and at the right time this connection was established. It was destiny!

Past experience also came in handy. I had managed several clients in my financial services days and had been closely associated with an IT Education company that used a franchisee model for its business. That's how I had built up reasonable experience in understanding the levers of managing this kind of partner relationship. This experience helped us build the first 20+ stores and a successful model that could be scaled.

Working with people like the Biyanis helped me develop an understanding of how retail worked, which in turn helped me steer Goli Vadapav to its destiny, despite having a financial services background.

As I recall our journey, I realise that everything fell in place all at once and since then I have become a firm believer that our life is nothing but our chase to our destiny.

> *'A breakthrough may take its own time to happen, yet when it does, things change forever. After Columbus, the world changed forever. And after Google, the world changed forever.'*

To quote Paulo Coelho:
'You have a dream.... The dream has come in the womb of the universe... it is the responsibility of the universe to fulfil the dream.... The universe conspires to help achieve your dreams...'

I could follow the trail back to a series of meaningful coincidences that occurred through my life.

A long time ago I attended Apooresh Acharya's sessions and asked him the meaning of 'faith'. In reply, he quoted an example from the Mahabharata: When Dushasana pulled at Draupadi's saree to shame and disrobe her, she held onto it with one hand and extended the other, calling out to Krishna for help. But did Krishna come? No, because this was 99% faith. When Draupadi raised her both hands for help, that was 100% faith and that was when Krishna came to her rescue!

CHAPTER 6

TECHNOLOGY

INSTINCT-BUILT GPS SHOWS THE WAY

Hindu mythology promulgates the concept of the divine trilogy. The divine three represent Creation -Preservation – Destruction in the forms of Brahma – Vishnu – Mahesh. As an entrepreneur, I have found this concept extremely useful, and it has helped me sail through many difficult situations.

In life, nothing lasts forever. What we create today, we will continue to build for a while. Our creation will continue live and grow but once it has outlived its usefulness, it will be destroyed. This is the law of nature.

Interestingly, destruction once again brings about something new. Something will be created again and this cycle of trilogy continues without end.

As an entrepreneur, what we create today shall be what we destroy sometime in the future. That will happen because my present creation would have served its purpose and must now make way for something new.

We built a magnificent infrastructure at an investment of

Rs. 50 lakh and created 25 branded vadapav stores. It was a beautiful creation in itself. We built it, watched it grow and we operated it, despite all kinds of problems. Yet now, it was time for a change.

Over the years, I have delivered over two hundred talks on the Goli Vadpav story. I am often asked how a big, established company like Vista Processed Foods entertained a small company like Goli Vadapav?

The same question was on our minds while sitting in a meeting with Vista for the very first time. At a later stage we came to learn that in those years, the company had unutilized capacity in their plant, although for the main part, it was Bhupinderji's passion to promote India's ethnic food.

'The breakthrough with Vista was a lucky one for us. After our first few meetings with Vista, I felt the need to check first-hand if this machine-made vada would work with our customers. I asked Vista to give me some samples for market testing. So they created some plain gramflour-coated potato patties and gave them to me in ten sealed packets of about twenty-odd patties each.

I told no one about this, but personally took charge of those packets and headed to Dombivili, to a hath-gadi-wala (handcart vendor). I gave him an advance tip of Rs 200 and a packet. I asked him to fry it, put extra chutney on the pav and give it to the customers. Then I stood at a distance to observe the customers' reaction. No one complained and in fact, some of them were delighted.

I repeated this experiment at as many hath-gadi-walas as there were packets with me. And when I saw that people had no complaints, I was sure Vista would work for us.

I did this in absolute secrecy and I am still not sure if anyone knows about this exercise other than Bhupinder Singh. That small experiment was a tremendous motivator for both of us.'

When the news of our tie-up with Vista reached the kitchen, the first reaction from the team was: what will happen to our jobs?

Yes, they had read it absolutely correct! This new tie-up would wrap up our central kitchen, making it instantly redundant. The fifty people working there would not be needed any more.

How could this be?

Most of our teammates questioned our decision. It was difficult for people to comprehend just why we were pulling down this wonderful infrastructure that we had created ourselves, with so much passion.

It was also difficult for us to explain that because we were now thinking of going national, this step had to be taken. Our vadapav brand would travel to every corner of the country and this was going to happen because we now had the technology.

So the vision that had driven us to begin this journey looked feasible, for the first time ever! We knew there were hurdles along the way but in principle at least, we had the best chance. And we realised this.

The procedure with Vista Processing Foods would take around three months to come into operation, and included getting necessary permissions from their Head Office in the US. In the meantime we had lots of work to do. Once again the paradigm-shift came into play with the actual shift being a series of procedures that had to be organised over these three months. From that point, everything we had been doing would change.

We had to understand the new requirements, and be ready to implement them. But we also had to continue running the business as usual.

Yes, we didn't close shop even for a day!

Thus, the trilogy worked in parallel!

Full credit for this transition goes to the team who took the challenge head on and delivered far beyond our expectations.

The three areas to experience the most significant changes in our value-chain were: (1) our central kitchen was to cease functioning; (2) we were to adapt to frozen logistics for our supply chain; and (3) we needed a new mechanism for frying vadas in the stores. Until then, like any other vadapav vendor the traditional kadai was our standard vessel for frying. However, now that

we were migrating to a frozen supplychain, we had to abandon this method as frozen products require a different kind of frying. Vista suggested that we procure fryers that McDonald's used in its stores. On inquiring, we discovered that they were extremely expensive.

We began looking for cheaper alternatives, but none that could be relied on for quality. So we decided to develop our own fryer.

Once again, I took the lead in this initiative. For this work I reached out to my old friend Prakash Jaikar, who has a habit of taking apart any machine he comes across. Much like Mr Funsuk Wangdu 'Rancho' in the movie '3 Idiots', Prakash was always found with a screwdriver in his pocket. Prakash was a qualified engineer from a leading engineering college of Mumbai.

One of the core Team colleague Mani, also had a deep passion for machines. I organised for the two to meet, and work began on the idea of designing a chip-based automatic fryer.

Now someone also referred me to a software guy who was on a sabbatical and on contacting him, he agreed to write the software for the chip, despite the fact that we had no money.

One day, my wife asked me how I kept finding people, and I too wondered about this talent. Years later on, looking back I realized that perhaps I was so engrossed in finding solutions for evolution that people seemed to pop up perhaps decoding my dream.

In those moments I figured that people with dreams were seldom bound by things like background, education, experience, etc.; instead they remained wedded to their dreams and would undertake anything that would help achieve that dream.

Thankfully, this time our experiments didn't fail. We created what we eventually called a 'Goli' fryer – a chip-based automatic gas fryer designed for frying frozen vadas.

Now frozen vadas needed an oil temperature stable between 170 degrees and 180 degrees centigrade for five minutes, to fry perfectly. When heated for the first time, our fryer reached 170 degrees in five minutes. An indicator on the panel would let us know when the fryer would be ready for use. An operator could program the frying time and then drop the frozen vadas into the hot oil.

The temperature in the pan would start rising, yet never cross 180 degrees. On reaching 180 degrees the burner would automatically stop, bringing the temperature down again through a flame control devise.

If, for some reason, the temperature dropped further, the burner would restart automatically on the temperature reaching 170 degrees. So the temperature would always be maintained at a stable point between 170 and 180 degrees centigrade.

If the designated frying time ended, the fryer would beep and at

> *'Technology always wins. A handful of Spanish sailors captured South America with one superior tool – the Toledo steel sword.'*

that point, the vadas would be removed from the oil.

Once out of the fryer, within two minutes, the vada would be packed between the pav at the assembly counter, to become a ready to serve vadapav.

By the time that process is completed, the temperature of the patty would further reduce to around 70 degrees level, the ideal temperature that a human tongue relishes cooked food. This is how we planned to ensure that our customers enjoyed an authentic hot, spicy and hygienic vadapav experience.

On designing the fryer, we realized that this could be an independent business in itself. The idea looked lucrative, and some of our team members were getting increasingly excited. But we insisted that we would remain focused on vadapav.

Vadapav was our passion and we were willing to walk every mile for it.

Subsequently, we hired a shed in Dombivili and began assembling our fryers there.

During our experiences in managing logistics for the business we had seen everything including the police station, court, lawyers and officials. While I had been busy searching for solutions to the problems of wastage, pilferage & non-standardization, in parallel, I was also thinking about this aspect.

While it was in my mind, I had no time or bandwidth to think deeply about this. In the meantime, Shiva managed the show with whatever we had.

But just before we met Bhupinder Singh and Vista Processing Foods, our problem solved itself. We had heard of frozen-logistics and had found the concept attractive. We felt it could help improve the shelf life of our product.

However, in 2006-07, frozen-logistics was a relatively nascent sector and there were not many players in that space.

Now in what may again be termed as a 'meaningful coincidence', standing at the bus stop near my home waiting to go to work, I entered into a conversation with someone from my neighbourhood. I knew this person was into logistics. In passing, I mentioned this challenge to him. He connected me to someone he knew and just a few days later, we had tied up with Jeena & Co for logistics support of our operations. I have this habit of talking to people and telling them my story, with interesting results!

While signing the contract, I asked their representative why such a big company would even consider buying out our entire logistics arm.

His answer left us smiling.

'One day you will be a big company too and at that time there will be ten competitors eyeing this account. Having come this far, I would like to capture this account right now,' he replied.

So even before we tied up with Vista, we had a logistics partner.

Jeena & Co was an end-to-end logistics operator for the food industry. The company transported items like ice creams, bakery products, vegetables, milk products and other products that needed frozen logistics. Though initially we didn't use their frozen supply chain, once we migrated to Vista Processing Foods, that integration happened seamlessly.

This little development also helped us in negotiating the initial rounds of talks with Vista. They informed us that we would be needed to upgrade our logistics support and we said we were already ready.

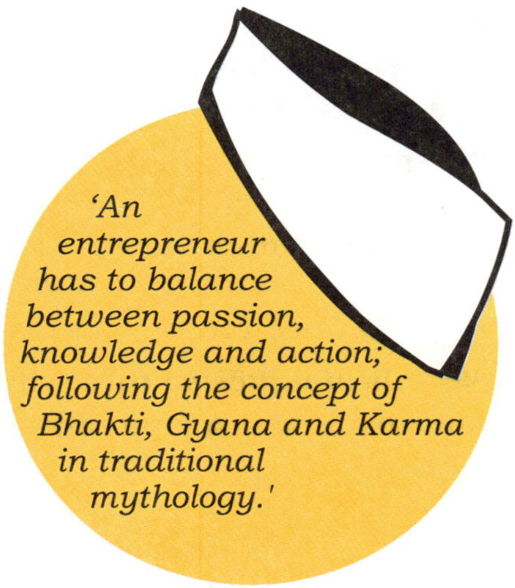

This created a very positive impact for both the relationships. Call it luck or chance, thanks to the association with Jeena & Co our requirements for Cold Rooms for storage also got resolved simultaneously.

But at that point we did one smart thing. We hired a refer van from one of our logistics partners and painted it in our colours to create an effect.

We are thankful to our logistics partners who allowed us this liberty at the cost of their own branding. As this was the only form of advertisement we had or could afford, it was an immensely critical move for us.

The tie-up with Vista solved the product problem of wastage, pilferage and non-standardization. The contract with Jeena & Co solved our logistics and storage problem. Creating the new Goli Fryer solved our frying challenge.

So only one problem remained from the supply-chain perspective. We needed equipment that could give us a stable minus 18 degree centigrade temperature for storage in the stores.

Hailing from Dombivili where every other shed manufactured something, we instantly began hunting for a solution. We discovered that the so-called assembled deep freezers used mostly by hotels and restaurants, could offer a maximum of upto minus 4 to minus 5 degrees of support.

Now our confidence was so high as we had discovered solutions through technology that we said, let's develop one for this challenge as well.

We had a kirana (grocery) shop next to our central facility and would occasionally saunter there to buy ice cream. On one particular day, about five of us were in the midst of a hectic brainstorming session on the minus 18 degrees issue, when we decided to take an ice-cream break.

We continued our discussion in the shop which was being

managed by a young boy, perhaps the owner's son or may be just an assistant. The boy was about 12 and he couldn't help overhearing our discussion. Suddenly he addressed us in a tone of absolute surprise saying, 'What are you all discussing, Uncle! This Blue Star freezer gives us minus 18 degrees!' He pointed to the freezer in the shop and began to laugh, amused at the thought of six blind men trying to guess the shape of an elephant by the part they touched!

With that it was time for our holiday with technology to end and for us to get back to vadapav, franchisees and the market.

So this is how we not only solved our problems, but made every arrangement to transition to the new system. We fixed every component of the value chain, at least in architecture. Then we shut down the old system and migrated to the new one.

By now we had resolved quite a few of our challenges, but one issue still remained unattended. We didn't know what to do with our excess manpower in our central kitchen. We had deliberately left this issue to be handled at the end of the process.

'At some stage we have to analyze our imagination to find practical solutions.'

We were very clear about what we would do with the actual infrastructure. As we would require a cold room of our own, we had decided to convert a part of the existing central kitchen into a cold room. We decided to let this space become our central cold room where everything would be brought from Vista, and then moved ahead from here for secondary distribution. Actually, this could be our big asset in the long run.

We had worked out this system, but were still looking for answers to the manpower issues. At this point, another very interesting thing happened.

Vista informed us that they wouldn't be able to prepare the masala for the vadapav. We would have to prepare it at our end and send it to them in drums before every production cycle.

Now the vada of vadapav is not a perfect product like a burger patty. Most Western foods have a coating of bread which makes it easy to manage on an assembly line using machines. In contrast, vadapav has a mix of spices like turmeric, which have strong colouring. Besides, the gram flour coating has a tendency to stick to anything it touches and can get fermented.

This is why Vista excluded preparation of the masala from their procedures.

And they had another reason: as our contract manufacturer, we were also asked to sign documents in which they guaranteed that they would not breach our secret formula.

Secret formula!

Yes, we knew that famously, CocaCola had one, and so did almost every leading brand. These formulas would be heavily guarded secrets and there have been huge stories around them. We had never imagined that our vadapav could have a secret formula, being of the view that it was already an open secret on almost every street corner of Mumbai.

But our partners had an absolutely divergent view and insisted that we must not just possess our secret formula, we must also protect it. And thanks to our international partners, we learned one of the most valuable lessons of brand building. We formalized our vadapav mix and the rest of our kitchen was accordingly, turned into what we now call our 'formula plant'.

This is how our old central facility was transformed into a production unit making masalas for the entire range of products. It also serves as the point of quality control and supervision for production purposes. Because of this move, we saved almost half of our manpower as our staff could continue in their jobs of preparing masala as they did before. So how could we utilise the rest?

Neither Shiva nor I were in favour of cutting jobs. All these people had worked extremely hard and it was because of them that we were at this point. We felt emotionally connected to all of them and despite many discussions, we always reached the same conclusion.

In the fight between head versus heart, it was the heart that eventually won.

Our financial position was still precarious and we knew that cutting jobs would be an excellent situation, yet we kept our staff. We decided that with all the changes to our system at short notice, perhaps we needed more people at the field level to assist our partners and as well as customers. So the rest of the team shifted from the kitchen to store-level operations and everyone had work, purpose and a path for career progression.

Most of the team responded to the change favourably. We explained that this was an opportunity for them to grow their profiles as individuals and professionals.They understood and welcomed the change.

But despite all the effort and care, some people didn't like the changes. A few agreed half-heartedly because they had no other option, but others who could not adapt to the change at all left voluntarily, to pursue other opportunities.

But we didn't cut a single job.

Finally, the day arrived when Vista started making raw patties for us. The trial lots of the product weren't received well by the team and most members felt that the product output wasn't appropriate. Some expressed their emotion and anger openly.

But I must truly thank the efforts of the engineers and technicians at Vista, who lived through the imperfections and immaturities many of us displayed during those initial weeks.

Shiva and I kept repeating to the Vista team that taste of the product was supreme to us and all credit to them for continuing to try until they had delivered exactly what we were looking for.

They had to undergo several challenges at their end. On one instance, their conveyor was ruined because of turmeric patches. On another occasion, gram flour paste caused blockage in the machines, and the entire plant had to be shut down. They faced all those teething problems, and yet delivered us the perfect product.

Perhaps if it had not been for Bhupinder Singh and his years of experience in the industry with advanced food technology, as well as his passion and perseverance to get it right, we might well have been lost midway through. But everything happened the way we had envisioned; and that was a big, big moment.

I still recall that first day when the assembly line was put on roll. In a big hall on one conveyor we saw burger patties being made for McDonald's and on the adjacent conveyor, vadas were being rolled for Goli Vadapav.

In a way, the symbolic meeting of these two similar looking twin brothers – Ram and Shyam – was a significant milestone on my journey!

So here's what Vista was doing for us. The first step of the process was potato washing, followed by peeling and dicing! Next came blanching at 100 degrees Celsius. This was followed by potato sorting and smashing.

The masala (secret formula) received from Goli Kitchen was then added to the smashed potato. The next step involved mixing of the two, followed by patty making or 'goli' making as it is referred to in traditional, unorganized vadapav-industry lingo.

On a subordinate line, the besan (gram flour) would be mixed with water and other ingredients, following the recipe. The besan batter then would be brought to the main line and patties would be picked up and dipping in the batter.

Patties (golis) coated with besan batter would then be taken to a par frying process for 30 seconds, immediately followed by freezing at minus 18 degrees for sixty seconds.

The next process was sorting of ready patties by checking for any visual or shape defects. Once this process was completed, the approved patties, 22 in number, would be counted and packed into plastic bags. Each bag would then be marked with a batch number, date of manufacturing and date of expiry for the stock.

Post packing, the units would be passed through weight testing and then finally, all the packets would go through a metal detector before being packed into boxes of 12 packets each.

The loaded cartons would be weighed once again, then marked and sealed. Once sealed, the boxes would be stored at minus 18 degrees Celsius in the cold room.

This entire process was conducted on a totally hands free HACCP certified process line.

From the Vista cold room, the boxes would be transferred to the Goli cold room in refer vans and as needed, Goli would distribute this stock to its stores via refer vans.

By using this procedure, the Goli product was at par with any FMCG or Global QSR product – like Britannia biscuits, Lays chips, Colgate toothpaste - standardized, hygienic, with a definite shelf life and an established batch trail.

What this meant was that if someone ate a Goli Vadapav in the remotest of locations and returned with a complaint, the company could now track the piece to the store where it was consumed, to the refer van that delivered it to the store, to the cold rooms it passed through, to the production report for that batch and the supervisor who had attended to it, to the 'masala box' that was used, to the potato lot that was consumed and finally, to the field from where the potato originated!

This was a definite game changer, and we knew it from the very first moment. In the process, vadapav had transformed.

The word 'enthusiasm' is derived from Latin;'en' means 'inside', and 'thu' means 'God'. Enthusiasm means invoking the God inside. Entrepreneurs have to be eternal enthusiasts.

I met so many people in my journey who told me my concept won't work. Our bankers asked us such tough questions, at times we felt like running away. But we persevered and because of this, we finally realised our dream.

I have heard professionals talking of the'4 Ps' - product, pricing, packaging and promotion. Now, I have observed that most people focus on packaging and promotion, but perhaps this is because those aspects were exciting. People would decorate their stores like McDonald's or KFC or Dominos, running media campaigns like these giants and wanting to own locations like them. They would create exotic packaging for their products, but this approach never attracted me. I always felt that these were secondary issues.

Maybe that's why we chose to concentrate on the product, feeling that if we got it right, 70% of our job would be done. When we asked the question – what makes a McDonald's, KFC or Dominos run thousands of stores serving millions of customers all at the same time across the globe; our answers were – no wastage, no pilferage, standardization and supply chain management.

So while most people looked at these chains from the frontend, I chose to see them from their backend. That is what made the difference for us.

Our belief was translated into confidence immediately, when the first batch of frozen vadas rolled out of the Vista conveyor. We realised we had been right and now had the first true chance of building a real brand around vadapav.

CHAPTER 7

FUND RAISING

VADAPAV GOES CORPORATE

In medieval times, the Arabs were an extremely powerful force. They spread from central Asia to Turkey in Europe, to North and East Africa and to India and beyond. They were fierce fighters and clever tradesmen who controlled most of the major trade routes of the world. For many centuries Europeans tried dominating them and failed.

That is, until Europeans discovered gunpowder.

Gunpowder was invented by the Chinese, but Europeans realised its firing power through the barrel of a gun. Today, that same power is ICBM – Intercontinental ballistic missile. This single piece of technology changed the face of the world over the next few centuries.

With gunpowder loaded in rifles and armed with guns, fierce Arab fighters were no longer a threat to Europeans, who could now attack them from a distance.

I have always believed that history teaches us some of the most valuable lessons. For me, history has always provided perfect inspiration.

The technology we discovered for making our vadapav was like finding gunpowder. It changed the complete direction of our business.

Once Vista started rolling golis for us, we had an interesting set of experiences within our team, in the stores and with our customers. The silver lining was that the customers liked the product. That became our benchmark.

Because the customers liked what they ate, the other participants in the value-chain had to accept this change. But it still took us over a year to match the taste of the machine-made vada to the taste of a street-made vada.

Once again, our policy of focusing on taste and taking the extra effort to get it right paid off handsomely. The team at Vista were perfect support for us in this area.

And Bhupinder Singh was like a coach for us. We learned a great deal from him about food technology, supply chain management and scale. He took initiative and gave us his unconditional support. All of these factors added immensely to our advantage.

Besides, he was the first person to take a risk on Goli Vadapav. He had to make investments at their end to service our requirements. He also supported us through our days of bankruptcy.'Don't worry, it will happen one day. You are on the right path,' he would say reassuringly from time to time, pumping up our confidence and self-belief.

In those days I felt as if we got the best from destiny. Now it was up to us to make something of it.

And so we moved to our next challenge – raising the first round of funding.

Now we knew that the banks wouldn't touch us. There was no gold remaining that could be pawned. There were no more properties that could be further mortgaged. (Yes, we had also mortgaged a couple of personal assets for interim funding). So, we had no option but to go to the market for the money.

So now we had something to talk about and a story to share thanks to our technology partners and their system of making vadapav on a world-class, hands-free assembly line.

Now we had to find an angel investor to put in Rs 5 crores to take the business to the next level.

While building this enterprise, I did some very strange things. One of them was drawing the profile of my ideal investor. So why did I feel the need to indulge in such an absurd exercise? People draw customer profiles, product profiles, but I drew an investor profile!

The point was that though everyone loved vadapav, yet it was a big challenge to corporatize it and make a brand out of it. I wondered how that could happen.

In India, IIT and IIM are considered extremely powerful brands and highly respected institutions. I felt that if a person with these educational qualifications or a CEO of a multinational bank invested in vadapav business at a good valuation, it would make the world take notice of vadapav, which was otherwise seen as a low end business.

I began the groundwork by scanning through the profiles of all top Indian corporates. Now this was before the social media scene and even prior to finalising our company's name, Goli Vadapav.

I had personally met many people on the list in the course of my work as an investment banker; some I had heard of, and few I had to hunt out.

Finally, I spotted one person whom I felt, was our ideal potential investor.

Now this also happened simultaneously while we were shutting our investment banking business and moving to Kalyan in 2003. So even before we had begun the venture, I had a profile of my ideal investor ready.

This may sound really crazy, but I actually did it. I made the choice based on the fact that this person had been CEO of a foreign bank in India. Following that he had setup an extremely successful BPO in India. He was well known and commanded great respect in the industry. In short, he had the clout and the glamour. Vadapav needed both.

I didn't know him personally, though I had met him on a few

social occasions. But none of them were one-to-one meetings he might remember. I had tried getting in touch with him through a source who worked with him, but nothing materialised. I then learned that he had moved overseas. Almost at the same time, we moved to Kalyan and launched Goli Vadapav.

One day many months later while things were progressing with the business, I learnt that an old friend was in a very senior position in the HR department of the BPO, which this model investor had founded. It was now early 2004 and we already had 8 to 10 stores operating.

With this information, I contacted my friend. I made his life hell! I did everything I could to get him to reveal my model investor's contact number.

My friend finally succumbed to pressure and shared his phone number.

Everyday morning, when I used to have my tea at Shiva's house in Kalyan, I use to dial this number and the call would go to a message box. I would leave a message after the beep 'This is Venkatesh from India. I want to know if you would be interested in investing in a vadapav company in Kalyan.'

Over the span of one year, I called that number repeatedly from Shiva's house every morning and each time my call went to the message box where I would leave the same message. And one evening Raji, Shiva's wife, called me up when I was in the store, that some Mr. Jerry Rao from US has called and was screaming, who is this person who calls me at midnight and tells Vadapav! Vadapav!...

At the same time I was busy with my search for technology for the business. And we had begun actively searching for money.

When we reached out to South Mumbai in 2007 we discovered that in a few years, the complexion of the finance industry had completely changed. A large number of investors who put money in new businesses (which were now called start-ups) were VCs & PEs.

While it wasn't difficult to make contact, yet our meetings would go haywire!

We realised we had two basic problems; the first was that people didn't know where Kalyan was located as their perception of India was IT, software, outsourcing, BPOs and Bangalore. Secondly, people didn't understand vadapav and had no idea of its importance and significance in Mumbai. Most of them had never tasted it either!

Thirdly, they didn't know 'Goli' as they were unfamiliar with the name and couldn't relate to what we claimed was our business, as part of our investor pitch.

After months of meetings with potential investors that were going nowhere, we realised that we needed something special to get to the right set of people.Our story just wasn't attracting investors, and it was becoming futile pitching to those people.

We also felt that we needed to find Indian investors in the market. Yes, these people were there, but perhaps we had not done enough homework in attracting them to listen to our story.

From our long experience in the business of finance, we understood that it wasn't going to work out as a matter of routine. So what could we do?

In the course of our meetings, we met a journalist and ended up telling him our story. When we parted, he asked us to look out for the next day's newspaper, and true to his word, Goli Vadapav featured in The Times of India.

At this point I wondered if we could have some important people validate our idea. "Luckily, I was able to get an appointment with an eminent face in the financial world, MD of leading private bank"

She liked our presentation and later her team visited us in Dombivili and Kalyan for due diligence as well. Unfortunately at that point, we had nothing to offer as security for a debt proposal.

Nevertheless, because one of the country's top bankers validated our idea, we gained more confidence and found an audience among the right kind of investors. In this sequence, one day we met Mr. Rakesh Jhunjhunwala (a leading stockbroker) who was very excited about our business. Similarly, Prof. Shivanand Mankekar (India's leading private investor) liked the project and wished to invest too.

When this happened, the validation had happened, but now we required valuation.

In the meantime, NDTV was doing a story on Mumbai food and found us. They visited our formula plant, saw what we did and soon, we were on TV!

We kept meeting more people, one name led to another. Following this sequence, we met Sujata Dabholkar, an old colleague and friend. When she heard our story, she placed a little Ganapati in my hand as a gift and said that she would connect me to someone who was sure to help us.

She connected me to Sanjay Kulkarni, who incidentally, was my ex-boss. Sanjay said that Sujata had spoken very highly of me and so he wanted to know what I had been up to.

We invited him to Dombivili and took him around our stores in Kalyan. He spent a good amount of time studying our business and understanding its nuances. I explained to him the kind of valuation I was looking at and he agreed to look into what he could do for us.

On the other hand there suddenly appeared a flurry of articles in the media about us, including regional publications.

Whenever I thought of people from my past who could help, I would call them. Now I approached another ex-colleague, Alok Bhargava who connected me to Ms. Neelambari Rao, a lady who did a lot of social work like teaching computers to lesser privileged children.

We had a very interesting meeting with Ms Rao. She heard us very patiently and made some very interesting suggestions. That was when we were still grappling with our manpower problems after dissolution of the central kitchen. Our people were in the process of rehabilitation and her experience in the social sector gave us quite a few insights on handling our situation.

Once the meeting was over, we thanked her and returned home.

In the meantime, Sanjay kept updating us on how he was pitching our story to the kind of model investor I had created in my mind.

Then one day, I got a call from Sanjay. There was great sense of urgency in his voice as he said Mr. Jerry Rao wanted to see us immediately.

Well, Mr. Jerry Rao was the owner of the phone number that I had been calling, the model investor who existed in my mind since 2003-04.

We jumped into a cab and reached his house when it was almost dinner time. Sanjay was already there, and at that meeting, Jerry Rao agreed to invest in us. It was pleasing to witness that Mr. Rao instantly saw the bigger picture of our business. He could visualize that we had the true potential to be a national chain. He understood that we had a wonderful chance to churn a national brand out of an ethnic food that had, until then, been restricted to the domain of the unorganized sector.

Besides, he said, at that point he was looking to invest into socially relevant businesses.

That evening we also discovered yet another meaningful coincidence - Jerry & Neelambari Rao were husband and wife! Incidentally, Sanjay received only a small part of our requirement as funding from Jerry Rao. But because Mr Rao had invested in us, within the next three days,one more corporate invested in us, finally giving us our quota of funds at the desired valuation.

As was expected, the deal made a significant splash within the investment community.

All our old friends, colleagues and associates from our financial services days figured that we were not 'giving goli' (bluffing) when we said we were getting into the vadapav business. And now, we had the top angel investor of the country, Mr. Jerry Rao and a few similar names backing us!

So now we had fresh money and new co-owners in Goli Vadapav Private Limited. We cleared off our major debts and went ahead with executing our cold room in the new formula plant, as planned.

But the end of one story is always the beginning of another.

We knew we had to scale up and felt that we could reach the number of 100 stores pretty quickly. We took this challenge as an opportunity. From the supply chain perspective, we saw no hindrance in supporting that kind of expansion and jump in operations.

'In raising funds, validation always comes before valuation.'

Now the Mumbai retail real estate sector was very hot – Subhiksha was growing, Big Bazaar was growing and Reliance Retail was growing. Amidst these expansions, there was no space for a vadapav store at ground zero. At the outset, landlords preferred renting their spaces to these retail entities.

When we said we needed a much smaller space, people preferred renting their shops to ATM providers, rather than renting to us. They saw vadapav as a messy issue that could spoil the ambience of their posh surroundings.

But withstanding all that, we managed to launch 8 stores at exorbitant rents, as showcase stores across Mumbai. We made sure that each of the locations was perfect from a retail perspective.

Whenever we faced civic and legal challenges while opening stores in Mumbai, we would approach Dr. Ramprakash Nair and he would resolve it peacefully. During one of our store inaugurations in Navi Mumbai although we faced some local trouble preventing our store launch, Dr. Nair was able to get the then CIDCO chairman to inaugurate the store. Once during a store inauguration in Mumbai when a local goon with strong connections was troubling us, Dr. Nair was able to get the then Director General of the Police to inaugurate the store.

But after setting up these, we took a break to look at the economics. We realised that it was not possible to open 100 stores in Mumbai, given the cost of real estate.

We thought deeply about this and tried several options. We even talked of partnerships and tie-ups, but nothing looked feasible or doable.

Just as we were about to drop the whole idea, we noticed the Aarey Milk Booths.

Aarey is a Milk Co-operative in Mumbai with over 1500 spots all across the city, on the footpath of every major road, to distribute milk to citizens.

We met the office bearers and they were instantly excited about the idea. Coincidentally, the person who owned the rights for branding and distribution was a very old friend – Jaipal Reddy.

This was how with one stroke, every impossible location like Peddar Road, Valkeshwar, Nariman Point, Gateway of India, Juhu beach area where several top movie stars live, and the posh Bandra sea-face, all these unique areas came within our reach.

On encountering this opportunity, we became overexcited! We lost every calculation, forgot our maths and just went for it! We did no risk analysis. We simply shortlisted 300 of the best locations and decided to launch all of them simultaneously, on a single day. Mani did a great job of completing the Aarey project work – decorating the booths with Goli branding and meticulously setting up the equipment like the refrigerator and the fryers.

And on this day, Goli became visible on every major street of Mumbai.

It was a tremendous logistical effort, getting 300 signboards, deep freezers, fryers organized, including an adequate number of refer vans to service these locations spread across the city. There was the challenge of training store operators, among other things. These were all immense issues, many of which we just overlooked in our excitement.

However while all this unfolded, we could feel that our dream of creating an Indian brand of mass consumption was finally materialising.

I thought of signing up a leading cricketer, whose love for vadapav was well known, as our brand ambassador.

And while all this was happening, somewhere without our knowledge, vadapav became a political subject in Mumbai.

An article appeared in one of the local newspaper and the very next day, we were in the midst of turmoil for all wrong reasons. Vadapav suddenly became a politically sensitive issue in Mumbai and the complexities that arose out of the situation proved too much for us to handle. We started getting threatening and extortion calls from local lumpen elements, there were unreasonable demands by the booth operators' Union, one of our existing stores got burnt down and it became very challenging to continue the Arrey booth operations smoothly. For various good reasons, our investors panicked. At that point we decided to exit Aarey and with that move, all the money we had raised went down the drain.

This misadventure also affected the existing stores in the city because of the working capital crisis. We had no money to pay salaries to our people, or pay the vendors. This led to a lot of chaos and conflicts within the organization.

People blamed us for destroying their careers and getting them into all kinds of unwanted troubles.

On the family front too, there were deep repercussions. My wife couldn't take the stress and had to be hospitalised. My daughter felt distraught. My father's health took a beating.

'Modern education encourages us to pass with flying colours and avoid failures. Entrepreneurship encourages us to try new things and embrace failures.'

I realised that in a span of a few months we had gone around in a complete circle, from being cashless to being cashless, once again.

'I have never seen someone burn Rs 4 crore in 4 months,' my father said. I realised that Rs 4 crores was spent at a big price!

Yes, that's what happens when entrepreneurs get carried away!

Goli Logo

Murbad Road, Kalyan

First Store, Kalyan

Goli Kitchen

Goli Van

Venky with Bhupinder Singh, CEO, Vista Foods

Goli Packet

Goli Logistics Van

Goli Fryer

Goli Vadapav Store Crew

THE TIMES OF INDIA

Mumbai's vada pav set to get American touch

Times of India clipping

सकाळ

• मुंबई • शनिवार • १९ फेब्रुवारी २००५ • दोन रुपये •

आता अय्यर पुरस्कृत वडापाव!

Sakaal clipping

ગોલી માર મુંહ મેં

Regional Media

Goli Arrey kiosks

REBUILDING

CHAPTER 8

STARTING FROM SCRATCH

It was a tough time but we still chose to look at the positives of the situation. Our model had been successful, our story was powerful. We felt that if we went back to the market and raised fresh capital, the situation could be brought back to life again.

Accepting our mistake and putting disappointments behind us, once again we approached the financial markets. This was September 2008 and as we began organizing meetings, things started gaining momentum. Then one morning, we heard the news, Lehman Brothers, the third largest bank in the USA had filed for bankruptcy.

Within hours of that event, money seemed to have evaporated from the market. There had been prospective investors in plenty looking to ride the wave of the India growth story, but suddenly none could be seen! Everyone was now busy covering their losses as a result of that one event in America.
Suddenly, we had no meetings to attend and whomever we called, said that they weren't looking to invest.

It was a very unusual period. I had never seen the kind of

silence I witnessed in the financial market during those few weeks in 2008, my entire career until then.

But we still didn't lose hope.

We stopped calling people and began meeting them. We simply kept pitching our story, again and again. We asked no one for money, we only shared our story.

Slowly, people began opening up to us. Things were slow, yet positive. We created some excellent pipelines and realised that now we had to be much more patient.

In January 2009 we were really close to clinching a deal in our favour, when something else happened – the Satyam and Subhiksha fiascos unfolded!

Following these two events, investors lost complete confidence in the market. All the people who had been talking to us and assessing us on merit-of-case basis, simply told us that they had put off their investment plans for now and terminated all talks with no further reason.

That was the gravest and the darkest hour of our journey.

We felt helpless! We had no money. Our old investors were trailing us. They put tremendous pressure on Sanjay Kulkarni, which spilled over onto us. My strength was completely depleted, I felt like I had no energy!

But at this lowest ebb, Shiva was full of energy and positivity! He has always been a crisis man, someone who can score 50 runs in 2 overs. In fact, he said to me,'This is the time to play,' he said, 'ab to khel ka mazaa ayega!' (Now the fun in the game begins!)

I couldn't understand what made him make that statement. Was he merely trying to cheer me up? But no, he meant every word he said. I recall his exact words: 'Let's not drop the bat. The pitch is tough and conditions unfavourable, but we will get a loose ball and that's when we will hit for a six!' He repeated with emphasis, 'Let's not drop the bat!'

I wondered what he intended doing. There was no money, nearly no team, no business and no leads. The only thing positive was that our company-owned stores were operational. Vista too, was still supporting us.

After the Aarey fiasco, most of our franchisees had been reluctant to continue with us and those relationships had to be terminated. The team had to be rebuilt, but how could this be done without money? But when I looked at Shiva, he moved as if he owned the whole world!

I remembered Paul Coelho's words from 'The Alchemist', that the language of the world is written in one word – courage, courage and courage. I witnessed this enfolding before my eyes. Shiva played an extremely courageous role. His practical acumen and understanding of the human psyche helped us steer things forward.

During the initial phase, especially post the Arrey fiasco our cash flow was always tight but we had a strong and cool CFO, Raji Menon who handled the challenge always with a smile.

The Aarey crisis had led to severe legal issues, and there was a winding up petition knocking on our door and once again our crisis man Dr. Ram Prakash Nair stood like a rock of Gibraltar with us; he took over the arbitration issue and resolved it peacefully.

It is said that when God closes one door, He definitely opens another. A businessman from Nasik had come to Mumbai on work and he happened to stop at our Goli store in Kalyan. A few days later he called us, asking if he could get a franchisee of Goli for Nashik.

Thankfully, Shiva offered him the proposition of developing the entire North Maharashtra region, as Master Franchisee for the whole territory.

The master franchisee received exclusive rights to build the region. He would appoint franchisees, get stores designed, constructed and launched, and guide franchisees in running them, select bakeries, procure pavs and manage the complete local supply chain.

Entrepreneurs are like jugglers. If material is available, there is scarcity of manpower, when manpower is available, there is scarcity of money, when the money comes, the market vanishes...

Our role was to ensure that the frozen product and chutneys reached Nashik and were made available on time.

This was a brilliant piece of re-engineering and through this one action, we transformed ourselves from a QSR company into a FMCG company. Our product was being manufactured by one party, a second was transporting it, a third party was our local distributor and finally, the fourth party was selling it. On our part, we were just co-ordinating the entire thing.

So with no resources or new investment, we spread our business to a new territory.

When the first Goli store opened on College Road in Nashik, we were welcomed to a different kind of customer experience.

In Mumbai, vadapav was food on the move. Fast food – finger food – mobile food! People ate vadapav for its taste and for its convenience. It could be picked up quickly without hassle, and was consumed on the move. In Mumbai, no one has the time and people are always rushing from one point to another.

Nashik proved to be a complete contrast. When we opened in Nashik, people saw the store as Mumbai's famous food coming to their city. They saw a brand coming into their town and an instant

'The journey of entrepreneurship is always a little ambiguous, making one confident and unconfident simultaneously. One may be confident of the car, yet not of the road. The road will need to be explored.'

buzz was created. People came to our store in their big cars with their families! They brought friends! They came to party, enjoy and relish the food at leisure.

At that time Goli Vadapav became a big phenomenon in Nashik. Surprisingly, we did not spend even a rupee's worth of publicity to make this happen. The procedure was simple. People came to our store, ate the product, liked it and inquired if they could get a franchisee.

Soon the movement started spilling outside Nashik, to other neighbouring cities. In every instance, we went through the same process and as a result in many of these new towns, we opened multiple stores.

The Nashik noise reached Aurangabad. A friend of the Nashik franchisee had multiple businesses in Aurangabad and the rest of the Marathwada region. He came to Nashik, visited all the Goli stores in the city and expressed his desire to be Master Franchisee for Aurangabad and the Marathwada region.

Goli opened in Aurangabad during the festival of Ganapati, with four stores launching at one go. The unit cost of the product was Rs. 8.00 at that point. On the day of Ganesh Visarjan, one of the stores did a cash collection of over Rs 50,000– over 6250 vadapavs sold in a day!

Once again in a short span of time, Goli Vadapav expanded deep into the entire Maharashtra Region.

Now while we had struggled to add stores beyond twenty in Mumbai, in Maharashtra we became a seventy-five store chain within a span of just one-and-a-half years.

“If nothing else, the Aarey fiasco had given us excellent visibility. The politicisation of Vadapav was covered by most of the media and they had also covered Goli Vadapav as a part of it. People now knew us. Most franchisees had seen us on television and had read about us in newspapers.”

Let me recall history once again. The Portugese started exploring the high seas to discover new sea routes to Africa and India in the early 15th century. To be precise, their first expedition left Portugal in 1412, to find a route to ports in Africa but their aim was always to travel to India and then ahead, possibly to China.

Until then, all trade from India and China was routed through central Asia, which was controlled by the Arabs.

Eventually in 1498,Vasco da Gama reached India and in 1512, the Portuguese reached China. It took them precisely a century to achieve what they had set themselves out to do, but they persevered and continued sending ships and expeditions to fulfil their purpose.

Countless voyages were lost, men died, captains were killed, mutinies happened, kings changed, yet they didn't stop. This persistence changed the course of history for ever.

Entrepreneurship is the journey of not stopping and always staying focussed.

So no matter what happened, we persevered with our vadapav dream and that is the distinction we can claim for ourselves, from this whole journey.

By the time we entered Nagpur, the complete picture had transformed. Goli Vadapav was now a brand across Maharashtra. We received excellent press coverage at our launch. The team led by Ajit Nair took the initiative and put in a great effort in expanding the brand across Vidarbha.

Entering into Nagpur was significant from two perspectives; firstly, we quickly extended our presence in the entire Vidarbha region, opening stores in all major towns and tourist locations. And once again, we could open more than a single store at each of these locations.

The second was that for the first time ever, we experimented with price re-engineering of the product.

Initially we were unsure about how the market would react, so we undertook an extensive study of the region. We discovered that vadapav was not the native food of these territories. We anticipated that people would come to us for a new experience; to relish food that wasn't their local cuisine.

The need for price re-engineering also arose because of the increased distance from Mumbai. Our logistics cost for taking the product to the location were far higher.

Nagpur introduced us to the science of geography-based differential pricing and that learning helped us engineer our strategy for the rest of India, which was next on the cards and still continues.

The credit for this understanding goes to one of our dear friends, Jabeez Muthala. Actually, after the Aarey fiasco when we were branded in the financial market as untouchables, it was Jabeez who listened to us. Jabeez had worked in a leadership position with a leading Private Equity firm for more than a decade and when we first met him, he was on a sabbatical. By then Aarey had already happened and we had no money, even for a day's survival.

Jabeez said, 'This is a Rs 100 crore business and it will grow to Rs 1000 crores. Don't give up!'

His words were soothing, but there was no money.

'We need money,' we said, nevertheless thanking him for his encouragement.

At that point he pulled out his cheque book and signed a cheque of Rs. 50 lakhs to us. The money came from his personal account.

We asked him what would happen if we were not able to pay him back ever.

'If you do well, return my money. If you don't, I will lose my money and that's okay. I believe in your story,' he said.

Jabeez contributed to our growth in several ways. He connected us with the people who were to become our future investors, more on that later. He boosted our confidence to venture into Bangalore. He introduced us to the science of 'bold-pricing'.

So when we opened in Nagpur, we launched at a different price-point.

Apart from this, there was no change in our strategy for this market. Our plans for expansion were always simple. We waited for people to come to us; when they showed interest, we demanded from our logistics team the promise to deliver in that particular region.

There was constant pressure on the logistics team to deliver and in the process we created frozen distribution facilities across Maharashtra.

We also had to create bakeries to make pavs in Mumbai style. Till then pav was a Mumbai and Pune phenomenon. We trained bakeries across Maharashtra to make 'Mumbaiya' pav.

By the close of 2009, we were a fairly transformed company. We were not what we had envisioned while starting off in 2003, but we were in a significant space.

One big difference from our early years, was the team. Initially we believed that we would build a core team and the rest of the organization would evolve around it. However, that didn't happen. After the Aarey incident, a lot of people at a senior level left and a few people within the existing team took on additional responsibilities to keep the show running.

Of course, Shiva was responsible to a great extent for motivating the team. But the personal contribution of each of our team members deserves full recognition. Many of them had no prior skills, experience or qualifications in the areas which they oversaw. Yet they accepted the challenge, going into the field fearlessly, facing the music, making mistakes, learning as we grew and eventually, they made Goli Vadapav what it is today – India's largest Ethnic Quick Service Restaurant Company - Winner of the Images Coca Cola Golden Spoon Award for Excellence in Food for three years (2013, 2014 & 2016). Goli Vadapav is the most admired fast food chain of Indian origin and Travel and Leisure rated Goli Vadapav as the 18th Best Fast Food Chain in the World, in its ethnic category.

Goli Vadapav is a start-up which has been written about as a case study in leading business schools of the world including Harvard, IMD Switzerland and ISB Hyderabad.

By late 2009 we had close to a hundred stores and the most interesting thing was that no one knew us in corporate India. That's because we had no presence remaining in Mumbai. People did remember the Goli story from a few years ago but perhaps many felt that we had disappeared since then.

At this point I wanted everyone to know that we were not a failure. Instead, we had become a magnificent success! We were expanding in Maharashtra.

Unfortunately, people didn't believe us. With no Goli store in Mumbai, the only memory people in the corporate world of Mumbai carried, were from the past.

That hurt me tremendously.

One of my friends felt that it was time Goli made itself visible to the investor community in a different way because he felt that it was only a matter of time before we would need funds to build infrastructure within and outside Maharashtra.

I wasn't very optimistic about the opportunity he suggested, but nevertheless, I took a stall at the TiE Entrepreneurship Summit in Mumbai in December 2009. The renowned 3-day conference was dedicated to entrepreneurship with more than 2000 delegates expected to participate from all over the world.

A few days ahead of the summit, I went to TiE's office in Mahalaxmi, which was abuzz with activity. When Manak Singh, Executive Director of TiE Mumbai learned that I was running a vadapav stall at the summit, he requested me to also include tea and bhajiya into the menu.

I smiled at the suggestion and told him that we were not ordinary vadapav people, as were seen on the streets of Mumbai. I explained that we made our vadas in a fully automatic HACCP certified plant run on world-class technology, where every vada went through an x-ray machine and metal detector. That's why I couldn't comply with his request.

As chief host of the summit the ED of TiE had thousands of jobs that needed his attention, and he was doing all of them perfectly. But despite that busy hour, after hearing what I had just said, he immediately called me into his cabin and asked me to relate my story.

Twenty minutes later he pulled out a sheet of paper covered with badly scribbled notes from the pile of papers on his cluttered desk, and picking up a pen, he wrote something on that sheet, which I thought might be someone's name. The next minute he asked me for my full name, wrote it down and informed that I was a speaker at the TiE summit.

I didn't react right then. I thanked him and returned home. A day before the summit, I went to the site in the Bandra-Kurla complex in Mumbai to take possession of the stall.

On reaching there, I was left aghast! Everything was in shambles. I had heard that the organisers were creating a venue since there was none in Mumbai that could accommodate so many people. I just felt that these guys were going to goof-up big time!

We had a new store opening in Marathwada, and I was to travel there. It would be better going to Marathwada than coming here the next morning, I thought. Now as my train was leaving in the afternoon I decided to show up at the venue since I had been invited so respectfully, and then I would silently slip off.

When I reached the venue the next morning once again, I was lost. The chaos of a day before had completely vanished! In its place was a beautiful conference venue with neat facilities for stalls, meetings and almost everything. The transformation was magical!

At the registration counter, I was quickly handed my speaker tag. I looked around and I saw the 'who's who' of the business world.

But I had no time to catch up with anyone as my team and I had to put up our stall. We had gone to the venue with a relaxed attitude, not expecting much. But nevertheless, we pulled ourselves together and quickly got our stall ready. Although in the process, my extremely casual attire became even muddier.

The conference was all set to begin, the chief guests began arriving. I left the finishing touches of the stall to my team and rushed to the main conference area just in time as the conference was inaugurated.

Since I was a speaker, a pilot spotted my tag and led me to the main auditorium. She dumped me in the only vacant seat in the first row. I was still surprised at the venue, wondering how they had managed to create that facility in less than 12 hours.

Still curious, I looked around and on turning my head to the left, I found this gentleman sitting besides me.

I realised instantly that there was something really wrong with my situation.

I peeked a little beyond and found someone else.

That's when I decided not to look any further! The cameras of the world clicked us unapologetically – Infosys, Tatas and Goli, seated next to one another. Within hours, these photos were all over the internet.

Somewhere during the session, Mr. Ratan Tata had turned to me for a moment and asked what I did. I said, 'I run a vadapav company.'

I had no idea what he would have thought about that, and there was no opportunity to find out as the proceedings of the summit continued.

Later when Shekhar Gupta, who was hosting the inaugural session with my neighbours, threw open the floor for the Q&A session, I was the last one to get the microphone and I put my question to Mr. Tata.

I had been burning from within, unable to accept that no one could recognise Goli's success. The investor community still talked of the Aarey fiasco, and they had alienated us.

'Entrepreneurship is about critical thinking, imagination and communication. Rice and lentil paste steamed as a cupcake is an idli; if spread like a crepe on a hotplate becomes dosa; and when fried in the shape of a doughnut is a medu vada!'

But the truth was that we were adding a store to our chain

every week! No one had the time to look outside Mumbai and enter into places like Nasik, Dhulia, Jalgaon, Aurangabad, Jalna, Beed and Nagar. So now that I had the opportunity to ask the last question of the summit in a place where all the best known global Indians were gathered, I took it head on!

Not long ago Mr. Tata had to withdraw from West Bengal, and not long ago we had to withdraw from Mumbai under somewhat matching circumstances. What were his comments on such kind of situations with reference to entrepreneurs in India.
The moment I asked the question, I sensed the buzz in the background and all around me.

The subject of political interference in business was a hot topic and my question was picked up by a few leading news channels. It was run on TV for rest of the day over and over again, giving us free visibility across the country.

I missed my train to Marathwada that afternoon. But in those three days, a host of people visited our Goli Vadapav stall. They included people like NR Narayan Murthy, KV Kamath, Nandan Nilekani, Kishore Biyani, Vinita Bali, Geet Sethi, Leander Paes, Rohini Nilekani, Kanwal Reiki, Sridar Iyengar and many other stalwarts who were attending the summit. Most important of all, we met our future investor - Sarath Naru of Ventureast.

Finally the Indian entrepreneurial community and the venture capitalists had heard the Vadapav talk while also relishing the delicious Goli Vadapavs at our kiosk.

I was a peaceful man once again!

CHAPTER 9

RISING FOOTPRINTS

MOMENTUM GAINED, FINALLY!

The peacefulness of an entrepreneur is in rising footprints. Finally, that moment arrived for us as well and we began gaining momentum.

A FMCG dealer from Bangalore was in Aurangabad for his principal company's annual conference, and he was selected as 'Best performer for the year'. As a reward he was offered a trip to Europe. That evening stepping outside his hotel, he stopped for a snack at a Goli Vadapav store in the city. Thereafter, a few days later he was talking to us in Mumbai about taking Goli to Bangalore, even before leaving for his vacation to Europe!

For sure we were excited, but simultaneously cautious as well. Our friend Jabeez had been already encouraging us to test Bangalore, and this enquiry came in parallel.

Would vadapav work in Bangalore? This was the big question. Incidentally not only in our minds, but surely in the minds of the rest of the members of the dealer's big united family that controlled his access to investment capital!

Logistically speaking, Karnataka was best suited to us for expansion. It was not as far from Maharashtra, and we presumed that it would have the available infrastructure needed to run our operations. Besides, Bangalore had already turned into a global city and the chances of acceptance of vadapav were really high.

Although we sensed the opportunity in Bangalore, our prospective partner's family were taking their time to come to a decision. They were trying to assess who we were, what we did and would the partnership be worth the investment. None of them had even known vadapav!

In March 2010, while we had been contemplating how to progress with Bangalore, fortunately I was invited to speak at a seminar in the city. Now a few journalists were attracted by our name and were interested in investigating what kind of a business Goli Vadapav was. They asked and the very next day, we were treated to a big front page story in the Bangalore Mirror.

This act of divine providence solved every problem at one go!

Our Master Franchisee took the paper to his family and friends, and they realised that vadapav was a serious business. I'm guessing that my photo with Mr. Tata and Mr. Murthy that also featured, also made a strong impact.
The result was that just a week later, we were preparing to launch Goli Vadapav in Bangalore at multiple locations simultaneously.

Ironic, in a way! Only a few years ago, an article on the front page of a newspaper had sent us packing out of Mumbai, and now here was another article that brought us into Bangalore.

Since then, Bangalore has turned out to be an excellent market for us and is in fact, the city with a maximum number of Goli Vadapav stores.

Thereafter we expanded quickly into other major cities of South India across the four states of Karnataka, Andhra Pradesh (now Telangana & Andhra Pradesh), Tamil Nadu and Kerala.

Later we entered North India and into Madhya Pradesh, Uttar Pradesh, Chhatisgarh, Punjab, New Delhi, Haryana; and thereafter the Eastern states of West Bengal, Orissa, Jharkhand and Bihar.

Once we delved deeper into southern India, it was delightful to see scenes of people wearing traditional Tamil veshti and foreheads decorated with vibhuti, digging into vadapav for a snack.

We had a new experience at every location we touched. Like in Coimbatore, the heartland of the Tamil world where life is all about idli sambar, thairr chatham (curd rice), and the women draped in silk saris wear kadamman (flowers) in their hair – we witnessed this culture settling down to eat vadapav! When we launched, we enjoyed a huge response.

In Raipur, people first expected dahi (curd) to be served alongside vadapav and still accepted us when we said we couldn't. The image of 'vada' in the North was that of 'vada sambhar' or 'dahi vada'.

All we said was try this new dish from Mumbai, and people just loved it.

Through vadapav we also experienced first-hand India's national integration – a Keralaite franchisee who spoke only Malayalam would get boys from Orissa who spoke only Oriya to work in stores; we sent a 'hand-holding' team from Mumbai who knew only Hindi and Marathi to direct them. Together the three factions worked to launch a new store. When this happened, I saw the real India - with all its conflicts, things could still work and the store would do great business and become successful.

Vadapav survived all barriers across regions and languages.

It was here in this period when we expanded our product range through a combination of in-house research and market feedback.

Initially we had just three variants - Goli Classic Vadapav, Goli Cheese Vadapav and Goli Schezwan Vadapav.

To this list, we added five new variants - Goli Mix-Veg Vadapav, Goli Masala Vadapav, Goli Makai Palak Vadapav, Goli Aloo Tikki Vadapav and Goli Soya Vadapav. We created a combination of spicy and non-spicy variants to address the multitude of customer demands for their tastebuds as they visited us from across the country.

Our inspiration for these products came from varied sources. When we saw spinach-corn sandwich and began wondering how this could be replicated in a vadapav format. Experiments in that direction led us to Goli Makai Palak Vadapav.

We surveyed the customer demographics and found that people liked spicy samosa. We asked ourselves what would recreate a samosa experience in vadapav, and that's how we developed Goli Masala Vadapav.

We also added two non-pav items to our menu, on popular demand. In Maharashtra people fast on certain days and have only specific food requirements during their fast. To cater to that segment in particular and customers in general, we added Sabudana Vada to our menu.

In Karnataka, people said that our menu had nothing for young children. We approached our partners, taking across a few options and recipes we had thought about, and they created a wonderful product for us - Cheese Ungli.

With these new products we once again tried to redefine the market, and our efforts have been successful to a great extent.

'When there's little money, one can learn to do things with a zero-budget.' And if there is no money, it helps being creative.

This was also the time when we mastered the art of frugal marketing and marketing via barter.

In 2010, we still had no money to spare for marketing and things had only begun returning to being positive;

plus we had to be careful too, yet we also needed to do something in this area.

One day, purely by chance we met a film producer who was making a Marathi movie. I asked him what he intended doing to publicise his film.

He had his standard set of answers. Once I had heard him out I asked if he would like the idea of putting posters of his movie in seventy shops across Maharashtra, at every location which catered to nearly 1000 people who came to eat vadapav every day.

He thought for a moment and then asked, 'What will I have to do in return?'

I requested him to shoot one scene of his movie with Goli Vadapav in the backdrop.

And this was how the Goli bus-stop was created in the film city of Mumbai and very kindly, he gave us two shots in the movie.

Subsequently we repeated the arrangement with several Marathi movies. Soon it became our big idea of generating publicity by barter.

We wondered how we could build the brand in Karnataka. As I visited Bangalore, I realised that there were a lot of people from Mumbai who worked there. They would visit our stores very frequently because they loved vadapav. So I decided to target them and make them our brand ambassadors.

But what could be done within the budget of a coin?

Then we had a crazy idea. We went to Kalyan railway station and put up a recorder close to the speaker on the platform. For three hours we recorded the announcements of train services in English, Hindi and Marathi, with the regular noise of the platform and sounds of the trains arriving and departing in the backdrop

'Platform number 5 par aane wali local 9:10 ki Mumbai Chatrapati Terminus jaane wali tej local hai... ... ...ye local ab platform no. 8 par aa rahi hai, kripaya yatriyon se nivedan hai platform no. 8 par chale jaaen.'

We then sent these sound clips to Bangalore. So while fine dine-ins and elite restaurants play soothing music, live bands and similar aural enhancements for their customers, we played the noise from the railway station!

When the recording went on air in the store, we couldn't believe what happened. People who had lived in Mumbai or hailed from the city went berserk with joy! An IT guy got so sentimental listening to those recordings, the very next day he brought along fifty of his co-workers and friends to listen to the real sounds of Mumbai. He said, "That's vadapav and that's Mumbai!"

'An entrepreneur must know where to benchmark - Mills & Boon or Shakespeare.'

For us, this was a brilliant discovery! Hence, thereafter wherever we went, we took along our Mumbaiya theme. This is how we then created cartoons, posters and such publicity material.

Later someone remarked that these ideas were good; yet the modern youth were not connecting to us as a brand.

We knew we could not go into malls, multiplexes and other cool places. But we did notice that a new platform had started surfacing over the horizon in those days.

'Facebook!'
It was new; it was attractive and the youth were taking to it and that was making big global brands sit up and take notice. The most handsome part of the package was that it was FREE!

Incidentally, Sanjay Mehta was an old friend and he now ran India's top social media agency. I went to him and he helped us set up our Facebook page. I told him we had no money to hire his agency, but we needed his help and he just laughed out loud.

He called our page: "Vadapav + Cutting chai + Amchi Mumbai = Awesomeness".

We posted our stories into three categories as 'Goli Gyan', 'Garam Goli' and 'Goli Gossip'. The idea was to talk about things that would tempt young people to 'like', 'comment' and 'share' what they saw on the page and feel associated with the brand.

In those days, in 2008 very few brands were using digital media and thus our efforts generated instant traction.

Sanjay suggested that it would be good if we started a blog, in parallel. Incidentally, there was no one I could go to for this task. Thus I took it upon myself. I started writing 'Vadapav Murmurings'. I didn't know what to write, so I penned straight from my heart, in my own style and from my own life.

At one point I became so passionate about this 'Facebook + blogging' thing that I would spend entire nights clinging to my computer. My father-in-law noticed my behaviour and one day, discreetly asked my wife to check what I was doing on the internet so late every day!

But that investment of time helped us immensely in enhancing the reach of our brand.

Now while all these aspects helped, other issues came to us by default. Perhaps our name was to be blamed for that. Bollywood became our natural support, specifically that one dialogue uttered by its most famous villain – Gabbar Singh in the movie of all times: 'Sholay' – 'Ab 'Goli' khaa!!!'

'Innovation happens when we question the status quo. Entrepreneurs find the courage to question the status quo in the face of long held tradition and belief.'

Actually, this expression was first uttered by a customer at one of our stores. Suddenly it spread like wildfire and at our stores, all our boys started muttering, 'Ab Goli Kha!!!' in perfect Gabbar Singh style.

Once all this happened, we

needed a face to create excitement and draw people's attention during our store launches; we found this in Balvir Chand, a lookalike of India's most famous cricketer.

He is a member of the Goli team and helps us with store launches and other BTL activities. This was another idea that was wonderfully successful over the past few years, in enhancing our brand power at the local level.

So, Mumbiya, Bollywood, cricket – what else did we have in our budget of a coin, to continue brand building?
Jingles!!!

'Khet gaye baba bazaar gayi maa...

Garam-garam 'Goli' tu khai le babua...'

We created several songs in various languages with the word 'Goli' included and played them at our stores and during events.

And while we were progressing on our path, somewhere here, the world also began to notice us. We had top business schools, including IMD Switzerland and ISB Hyderabad writing case studies on us. Later Harvard started teaching the Goli Vadapav case study to their students.

We received a few awards and recognitions on the way as well. Goli Vadapav won the Images Coca Cola Golden Spoon Award for Excellence in Food for three years (2013, 2014 & 2016). It is the most admired fast food chain of Indian origin and Travel and Leisure rated Goli Vadapav as the 18th Best Fast Food

Chain in the World.

And through this combination of opportunities, we kept our brand ticking and growing over the years.

The next interesting part of our journey was raising money for the second round of funding, which unfolded in a very interesting manner.

Soon after the TiE Summit in 2009, I began receiving invitations to talk at conferences and business schools, and share the Goli story. The talks went on adding to the buzz about us in the market. I spoke at more than 250 conferences, summits and institutions including IMD Switzerland, Harvard, ISB Hyderabad, Loyala College, SP Jain, Symbiosis Pune, Welingkar, etc.

The press would write about us very often, and we featured on several TV shows. TiE once again invited us to attend its Annual Summit in 2010, in Delhi.

Press coverages definitely helped in creating a conducive environment for our brand and we also had a plus point - the strength of our balance sheet.

Also by 2011, the markets had revived substantially and the number of Indian funds had increased significantly in the market. Investors had also started recognising potential within the food industry as the success of Café Coffee Day and public issues by Jubiliant Foods and Speciality Restaurants made the pitch favourable for the entire industry.

In August 2011, Goli Vadapav raised Rs. 21 crore in venture capital funding from Ventureast, a leading India-centric venture fund.

The investment announcement made news in the media and also marked the beginning of a new chapter Goli Vadapav's journey.

Goli stores in interior Maharashtra

Goli Vadapav

Cheese Finger

Cheese Vadapav

Schzwan Sabudana Vada

Sabudana Vada

Makka Palak Vadapav

Goli, Tata, Infosys

Venky, Shiva and Sarath Naru

BANGALORE MIRROR

THE SUNDAY READ

ON THE 'GO'LI

What's in a name, you would ask. But it may mean a lot of things to different people, especially when you have a company with a name like Goli Vada Pav. S Venkatesh of Goli tells that it is all about being "Mumbaiyya" and Indian

Bangalore Mirror

Veshti, Vibhuti and Vadapav in Coimbatore

Pepsi Truck back

Goli Mumbai Theme

Goli in Movies

Goli Man

Balli at Store Launch

Goli at Harvard Business School

Goli at IMD Switzerland

Goli at ISB Hyderabad

Goli at TiE Delhi 2010

Goli at Kotak

Ventureast Funding

Business Today

Coca Cola Golden Spoon award

Goli New Stores

CHAPTER 10

THE JOURNEY CONTINUES

When Ventureast invested in Goli Vadapav, for the first time ever we had a real budget for product development, market expansion, team building, marketing and brand building.

Yet we didn't splurge.

In this sense, Ventureast has been a good partner to us over the years. Most importantly, they supported us in our core beliefs and helped us consolidate our philosophy of design.

I have always believed that in any business, its design is the most important component. If the design is good, the business shall work.

In our case, when we started Goli Vadapav, we knew little about the food business. So we went to the experts and shook hands with them. That was our design.

Starting from our first team of kitchen boys who taught us how to operate the kitchen and get the taste of Indian street food right, to our logistics partners and Vista Processed Foods, at every stage we partnered with experts. This was our design.

Thereafter, each component of the business was designed to bring momentum to the whole process.

The vada was made by a specialised entity; logistics was managed by experts in logistics, the pav came from a local bakery source, the chutney was made by special sauce makers, and the franchisees were investing in the business and making it successful.

All this was part of the design.

Some time back when I was invited to ISB Hyderabad, I heard Prof. S Ramakrishna Velamuri who prepared the case study with Sonia Mehrotra and was teaching the case, offering a wonderful analogy by quoting the example of Amazon. “Amazon played with the design of the business, and brought technology and logistics into it and revolutionised the book business. Otherwise, the customer was the same. The customer had been buying books for ages. Thus there was no change in the product, yet Amazon changed everything by altering the design of their business,” he stated. The professor further said that we did something similar with vadapav. “The product was the same we brought in technology,

logistics and franchising to vadapav and vadapav became a national phenomenon,"

Prof. Anand Narasimhan and Aparna M. Dogra of IMD Switzerland did a case study on Goli Vadapav and invited me to give a talk. While lecturing the students, Prof. Anand Narasimhan defined us as the 'Hollow Organization', a term they use to define companies that grow by retaining least of their components in-house and instead, choosing to develop themselves through outside support.

Both the researchers who wrote the paper, felt our design was the reason for our success. It was simple to multiply.

I had always felt that true entrepreneurial conviction comes from the design of the business model, and in this reference I was always very clear in my mind about Goli Vadapav's design selection. I never had any apprehensions in my mind; I faced no fear and that in turn, formed the foundation of all my explorations over the years.

So even though I was unsure about the markets and their price points, I was absolutely confident of this idea working for us. And though I had no clue where the big breakthrough would happen - in Mumbai or in Bangalore, - I knew it would happen for sure!

After Ventureast came on board we started working on new store designs, POS, analytics, recruitment, sales and operations.

On the sales and operations front, we had a passionate and committed sales coordinator in Asha, my wife. She had spent her entire work life is sales and operations. I always saw her as a ten headed Goddess Durga coordinating for logistics, production, new product launches, induction and training simultaneously. Her phone would start ringing at the breakfast table with the regional sales team and would not stop before midnight. The calls would be about a big sales number in a large event, or a newly launched store sales or a new product breaking records or the anxiety of meeting the month end sales targets. I would often ask her to stop it when it continued beyond midnight and she would say 'sales and operations is the heart of the business, the heart can't stop.'

Yet, we know that the world celebrates hunters and explorers and makes them heroes. They are the ones who scale new horizons, find new lands and discover new things. They are widely cherished and often remembered.

Hunting, exploring and discovering are exciting, however, it is the task of farming - boring work that requires discipline, repetition and patience - that brings sustenance to civilization.

It is the farmer who tills the ground, grows the crop, puts in the silent effort and it is these actions that bring to the world wheat grass to feed our bellies.

Civilizations and empires are built around farming. Similarly, businesses and enterprises are built around operations.

For us at Goli, whatever has

happened till now has been more of hunting and exploration. So from this point, our future lies in farming; operations will be the new Goli.

Operations is a different challenge, it is way more difficult and requires deep patience. Besides, there are no visible heroics in it.

We know that what we have done until now has been only the art of the business. From this point, we are working on the science of business.

Our business is about bulk buying, bulk producing and bulk selling. We have to plan, purchase, produce, move and sell.

The science of our business is in market-related products, pricing, promotion, training and processes.

I believe that entrepreneurs are explorers; they seek to create new things from their imagination. And of course, they often end up leaving behind a bit of a mess, a touch of confusion. And this is precisely why entrepreneurs need professionals.

'Sales and Operations is like a wild animal that needs taming. Spot it, capture it and through trial and error, work out the best way to win its trust.'

It is professionals who organise, convert chaos into order and they achieve this through structured operations. Every start-up reaches that point of inflection in its journey when the meandering explorative path of the entrepreneur must transition to the structured methods of professionals.

At Goli, we are now at that stage!

Just like human civilization has evolved from the age of hunters to farmers to industrial to information, Goli too has evolved from the age of the kitchen to the product to franchising, and is now at the operations age.

Goli created the Vadapav category nationally by opening more than 300 stores across 100 cities of 20 states, and vadapav became a big food category across India. Many brands like Wal Mart's Best Price, Godrej Yummy Vadapav and other smaller manufacturers and distributors started following our example.

Goli started facing challenges on cost and competition, and the power of the product was being challenged. We realised that we need to shift from power of the product to power of the brand.

We are now in a phase where we must move from the power of the product, to the power of the brand.

In our journey, we have created an excellent bandwidth for our business. We have extended into 100 cities across 20 states across the dimensions of our beautiful and vibrant country. We have set up a robust delivery network and have been able to service customers successfully in every location.

In that sense, we have been very similar to any FMCG business, which operates through a large base of distributors and thrives on the efficiency of its inventory management systems.

Our growth occurred because we could successfully deliver our product to our distributors (franchisees), who in turn served the end customer at the last mile. Correspondingly our team has comprised of mostly home-grown professionals specializing in vital areas like vendor, logistics and franchisee management.

A persistent focus on these 3 domains has brought us to this point in our story.

Now for the next level of growth, our task is to co-create depth in our business, which means fostering customer centricity, enhancing customer experience and aspiring for customer satisfaction and delight.

An extremely important part of our business is the franchisees who run the stores, as their involvement in the business is translated into customer satisfaction and delight through the excellence of their operations. A lack of involvement in the business by the franchisee will result in lower sales, making it difficult for us to remain in business. To address these issues and make the process a robust one, we have professionals who manage relationships with the franchisees and appoint operators to help them excel. They also suggest renovation or relocation of the stores according to the needs of the business.

'When franchisee investment has happened, the next challenge is franchisee involvement.'

I will reiterate, the food business is all about taste and if there is anything beyond taste, it is the customer experience.

So while in our first phase we grew on the strength of the taste of our product and our distribution network, we now have to look at enhancing our service and consumer experience as our dimension of strength, similar to how all leading brands of the world in the food and the QSR industry develop themselves.
To achieve this we have been adding fresh arms to the set-up of our existing team. While this transformation is happening in a natural manner, we have observed that two things are happening simultaneously.

On the one hand, our existing team members are acquiring new skills to rise up to the new challenges of changing times, but we are also seeing experienced professionals from the multinational FMCG and QSR industry joining us.

This joint evolution is what will shape the next phase of our story.

'Success lies in managing the width and depth of the business simultaneously.'

I have an interesting hypothesis: shareholders of the company earn their dividend or interest; employees earn their salaries; franchisees and distributors get their commission; vendors get their payments. All these people are only taking something from the company. So in contrast, it is only the consumers who are paying into the company!
I try to convey this truth to my team

as much as possible. It is our job to service our millions of customers across the country through our points-of-sales, collect what they offer us as revenue, and work out the best way to distribute it fairly between all the stakeholders.

This I believe, is the operational test for the new team.

At this level we are looking to be driven by a six-layer structure encompassing following points:

1. Sales Review Process
2. Loss of Sales Monitoring
3. Operation Excellence and Training
4. Catchment Penetration and Local Area Marketing
5. New Product Launch
6. New Business Channels

Eventually in our business, the route to customer satisfaction is straightforward; it comes from serving a hot, spicy and tasty vadapav. This is one thing we are not going to change, ever!

> *'Exploration – Exploitation – Evolution, are all connected. The British built railways, post & telegraph, modern education system, judiciary and law & order, which later became the foundations of modern India.'*

'Rome was not built in a day' is a popular saying which is also true. The Roman Empire was one of the biggest empires in the world, at one time encompassing all of Europe, North Africa and Asia Minor.

If we trace their reach via a modern map, 55 countries from Europe, Africa and Asia Minor were part of the Roman Empire!

The Romans built the best roads and highways, canal and sewage systems; and were renowned for their astounding architecture which started with clay and ended with marble, with many ancient structures still standing today. They made huge strides in military, legal and civil issues, and their armies marched forth, conquering new territories.

At the time it was thought that the Roman Empire would last forever, but at its peak, Jesus of Nazareth arrived on the scene and changed this scenario. At some point, the Romans gave up their Pagan Gods and embraced Christianity. Following this, the Catholic Church became a powerful institution, wielding tremendous power.

It seemed like Christianity was firmly entrenched in Europe but around the 7th century the Prophet Mohammad gained significant followers in the Middle East, converting most of the region to Islam.

The Mongols, Turks and Mughals from Asia under the banner of Islam, spread to major parts of Asia and Africa; they entered Europe via Istanbul and Spain. It seemed that it would be only a matter of time before Islam would rule Asia, Africa and Europe

But Portugal and Spain used the oceans, a sea route to India, to gain monopoly of the spice trade that had always travelled West over land, which was now completely controlled by Islamic rulers.

The Portuguese discovered India, the Spanish discovered South America and trade on these routes was established, making these countries fabulously wealthy.

At the same time, Britain, France and others joined the race, establishing colonies in South and North America, Africa and Asia. Britain became Great Britain with a strong reach of colonized countries under its mantle and was soon the most prosperous and powerful country in Europe and the world.

But history is full of twists and turns, so after two World Wars, a beleagured Great Britain gave way for the rise of two superpowers at loggerheads with each other - the USA and the USSR (now Russia).

> *'America is moving into the imagination age with companies like Apple, Google, Facebook, Whatsapp, Tesla and Spacex, among others. It is now outsourcing its industrial age and information age.'*

The world has progressed since then and now in the 21st century, we face other challenges.

As we entered the 21st century, companies and brands from the USA and Europe had already begun outsourcing manufacturing to China and information analytics to India. India has jumped directly from the agricultural age to information age and somewhere skipped the Industrial age.

The information age boom and the subsequent phenomenal success of companies like TCS, Infosys and Wipro followed the liberalisation process that begun in India in the early 90s. This led to exponential growth in the Private Banking, Insurance, Telecom, Retail, Infrastructure and E-Commerce sectors.

Now for the first time in several centuries, the world's attention has returned to India, now being hailed as one of the most rapidly emerging global economic powerhouses.

Can this truly happen to us?

Can India sustain 8% GDP growth and a 25000 stock market index? Can we sustain growth by only providing information analytics to large American and European companies?

The fact is that because of wage arbitrage, Western countries can easily shift their loyalty elsewhere, using the services of other Asian, South American or East European countries.

Economies like the USA are built on brands like Gillette, Coke, McDonald's, Walt Disney, Wal Mart, Citibank, IBM, Windows, Apple, Amazon, Google, Facebook, etc.

India is a consumption story. We are at that point of time in history where many things have worked for us and now as a nation, if we don't clutch the opportunity with both the hands and erase the curse of poverty from this part of the world, history may never forgive us.

And for this to happen, we need brands that will create education, employment and entrepreneurship at the bottom of the pyramid. Goli Vadapav on the backend is connected with the farmers and on the front end with the store boys, who serve vadapav to the customers. The business start with the rural poor farmer and ends with the urban poor boy. And tomorrow when Goli Vadapav moves from 300 to 30,000 stores, wealth will not only be created but also get distributed.

And when hundreds of brands like Goli Vadapav across various industries become successful, the dream of India becoming an economic superpower will be realised.

I firmly believe that this is the direction of our future

journey. And I invite all entreprenurs to share this vision and join the journey, making it your own.

In conclusion, I retierate the five milestones in our goal of corporatising vadapav and finding it a place among the burgers and pizzas of the world. First, signing up with Vista Processed Foods and obtaining world-class-technology for vadapav.

Second, bringing investors like Jerry Rao and Ventureast into the business, giving it corporate respectability as a business venture.

Third, our franchisee partners who believed in our story and built Goli stores in 100 cities across the country.

Fourth, the team that built Goli, each person who contributed to its chapters which has allowed me to share this story with the world! Without them, there would have been no story!

Fifth, and this happened on its own merit when top B-Schools like Harvard, IMD Switzerland & ISB Hyderabad researched and wrote the Goli Vadapav case study which is taught to the students in their curriculum.

Beyond this we have millions of customers who have very gratefully honoured us by enjoying their Goli Vadapav every day for all these years, and all over the country.

We have created a network of 300 franchised stores across 100 cities in 20 states. We also have a strong team of professionals from multinational FMCG and QSR companies. like Unilever, ITC, McDonald's, KFC, etc.

We are facing new challenges and evolving. There is a lot of work to be done on Location planning, Franchisee selection and engagement, Operation Excellence, Training, Catchment penetration and many more... But most important of all is the Goli Academy – sourcing and training store manpower... ... at this juncture I'd like to quote Robert Frost ...

"The woods are lovely, dark and deep,
But I have promises to keep,
And miles to go before I sleep,
And miles to go before I sleep."

To all of you, I say,
'Picture abhi baaki hai... mere dost!'

GOLI NEXT

By Rajiv Prakash, Next in Advisory Partners

Goli's vision is to become India's McDonald's, not just for India, but also from India for the world. We have so far seen how Goli took Mumbai's signature dish, "Vadapav" national. And how! 300+ stores, across 100 cities and towns in 20 states across most regions in India and 20 million Vadapavs a year. In this process, it has made Vadapav a much-loved, anytime, anywhere snack for millions. These millions are consumers from all socio-economic segments in urban and rural India. And this consumer loyalty has been won by a good product, and not outrageous discounts and extravagant promotions.

Goli's success presents rich learnings in product management, production, distribution, sales and marketing. Combine these with Goli-style design thinking, frugal innovation and risk taking, and we have a playbook for any consumer entrepreneur seeking to address India comprehensively. Truly these have not been without challenges, some near-fatal.

So this is the inspiring view of Goli's start-up journey in its rear-view mirror. The windshield view is all about scaling up. And that's what Venky means, when he quotes SRK and says

"Picture abhi baaki hai mere dost!"

Goli is now at the very exciting next stage of getting closer to its vision – from starting up to scaling up. With numbers and market coverage mentioned above, one can't be faulted for thinking that Goli has already scaled. During my stint at Future Group, when we were tempted to pop the champagne too soon, Kishore Biyani would remind us that the Indian consumption market is huge and entrepreneurs/consumer marketers should think and act bigger. Imagine India as a billion consumer country, he would gently admonish.

So what's the context for the scaling-up? Can Goli become a million transactions a day brand? Can it become synonymous with the snacking category, especially the "char baje ka bookh" and beyond? Why think only India – if India can embrace pizza and pasta, can't Goli's Vadapav conquer palates and hearts overseas, from Western markets to Far East? With home delivery and online ordering penetrating food in a big way, how can Goli use this

ENTREPRENEURSHIP AND QUANTUM PHYSICS

Entrepreneurs focus their energies on certain thoughts, and those thought energies manifest as matter in the realm of space and time.

channel to make a Vadapav available anywhere, anytime? And can't Goli become one of the top QSRs globally? Audacious? yes. Ridiculous? no. These are not just speculative, crystal-ball gazing questions. On the contrary these explorations represent real short to medium term opportunities for Goli today.

Take sales channels, for instance, where Goli is pursuing a mix of depth and width strategies for breakaway growth. Depth focuses on operation excellence, new product launches and intensive marketing. The resultant same store sales growth could double sales as per these plans. The width strategy encompasses growing tier 2/3 city presence from 300 to 1500 stores, 500+ stores in tier 1 cities with innovative models to address higher rentals, integrating digital channels into the core of the business, and harnessing ready networks such as railway stations, petrol pumps on national highways, BPO and IT parks. These plans, if executed and funded well, have the potential to deliver 10X growth in 4-5 years.

So it's September 2016 now and Goli sees ahead a rich spectrum of opportunities, successful execution of which will take the company close to its dream of becoming India's McDonald's. Over the past two-three years, Venky has been focusing heavily on evolving from a start-up to a scale-up to get ready for the next orbit. Facilitating a change in internal thinking about the need for organisation and professionalization was an important first step. How do you distinguish between a good cost and a bad cost was a question often asked, given Goli's inherent frugality and the gestation period of such investments. Another consideration was partnering with franchisees whilst driving change. Yet another often asked question was whether such change would damage Goli's unique culture.

So over the past thirty months, after several iterations, Goli now has in place a strong cadre of sales and marketing managers from reputed QSR and FMCG firms, management systems for business and individual performance, active technology at the front-end and back-end, a revamped product portfolio, tested and formalised business processes and valuable lessons learnt on same-store sales growth, managing risks in a network organisation and the importance of branding.

These are important foundations for scaling-up but the orbit shift will never be linear. Numerous challenges will be faced both in the market and internally. And then we have the personal transitions for the founders as they seek to grow to the next level of leadership. Goli has always grown with partners and this phase may bring in more such strategic associations. Some fundamental assumptions about the business model too may get challenged.

But then, challenges are not new to Goli's founders. Venky's favourite analogy is Amitabh Bachchan, rising up after a big fall and emerging victorious. To Venky, Goli's scale-up is his next start-up with motivation levels similar to when he and Shiva started out. That said, he is realistic that nothing can be taken for granted, including Goli's earlier success formula. Whilst success is never pre-ordained, I see Goli as being well-positioned and ready to jump to the next orbit. When that journey pans out, we would well have enough and more for 'My Journey with Vadapav – Part-II'.